Blessings
from
The Other Side

Also by Sylvia Browne

Life on The Other Side
The Other Side and Back
Adventures of a Psychic

SYLVIA BROWNE

with Lindsay Harrison

Blessings *from* The Other Side

Wisdom and Comfort from the Afterlife for This Life

BOOKSPAN LARGE PRINT EDITION

A DUTTON BOOK

This Large Print Edition, prepared especially for Bookspan, Inc., contains the complete, unabridged text of the original Publisher's Edition.

DUTTON
Published by the Penguin Group Penguin Putnam Inc., 375 Hudson Street, New York, New York 10014, U.S.A. Penguin Books Ltd, 27 Wrights Lane, London W8 5TZ, England Penguin Books Australia Ltd, Ringwood, Victoria, Australia Penguin Books Canada Ltd, 10 Alcorn Avenue, Toronto, Ontario, Canada M4V 3B2
Penguin Books (N.Z.) Ltd, 182–190 Wairau Road, Auckland 10, New Zealand
Penguin Books Ltd, Registered Offices: Harmondsworth, Middlesex, England
First published by Dutton, a member of Penguin Putnam Inc.

ISBN 0-7394-1523-9
Printed in the United States of America

This Large Print Book carries the Seal of Approval of N.A.V.H.

from Sylvia:

Especially for my two sons,
Chris and Paul,
who, by being such wonderful parents,
pay me the highest compliment
a mother could ever receive

from Lindsay:

For Dad, who I know is watching
and to whom I owe a dance.
And for Mom,
who will always be my hero.

Contents

Acknowledgments

From the bottom of my heart, I want to thank every client through these many years, every viewer, every listener, every audience member, and everyone who's ever written to ask me for help, advice, or just a moment of comfort when their hope was running low. I may not remember your names, but I'll never forget all you've taught me and all you've brought to my life by inviting me into yours.

You're in my prayers, and I cherish you.

SYLVIA

Blessings
from
The Other Side

Introduction

I am blessed, there's no doubt about it. Despite its inevitable bumps and bruises, I love my life. I love my career. And the best part of all is that there is no separation between the two. Every day is filled with my children and grandchildren; my ever-growing menagerie of pets; my staff and ministers, who are as much my family as if we were related by blood; my dear, close friends; clients who instantly feel like friends; trips throughout the world with people I love by my side; regular television appearances with my best friend, Montel Williams, and other brilliant, fascinating people; and certainly my writing, which has been one of my greatest passions since I was a child.

But as odd as this might sound, nothing satisfies my frequent need for a real "intimacy fix" quite like my lecture tour. At first glance, *intimacy* might not seem like an appropriate adjective for standing at a microphone in front of three or four thousand people. I assure you, though, intimate is exactly how it feels to me. It's not just the fact that on any given night I might be hopelessly upstaged by my seven-year-old granddaughter, Angelia, performing a spontaneous, unscheduled dance routine to the delight of the crowd before I've even been introduced, so that nine times out of ten my entrance is almost beside the point. Or that I might be in the middle of answering a heartbreaking question from the audience about a missing loved one when, before anyone can stop him, my two-year-old grandson Willy could stroll casually onstage eating a bagel, just to say hi. Or that, because it's all live and unrehearsed, whether it comes from me or from the audience it's almost anyone's guess what might happen next, the possibilities ranging literally from the utterly ridiculous to the utterly sublime.

No, for the most part, the intimacy comes from my knowing that every audience, no matter what city or state I'm in, will create a unique, intensely personal atmosphere all its own, and because I naturally react to that atmosphere, each lecture is a whole new experience, for me and for the audience. It comes from looking out not at a crowd of strangers but at row after row after row of open, sincere, expressive individual faces that become very familiar to me by the time our hours together end. It comes from seeing the legion of Spirit Guides, Angels, and departed loved ones who invariably accompany every person in that room, eager for this opportunity to be acknowledged. It comes from the silence of a meditation, the laughter of an unguarded moment, the relieved tears of a long-awaited answer, and the fact that we all share every one of those surprises together. It comes from getting back every bit of love and energy I give and then some, so that by the end of a lecture I've been presented with the gift of feeling stronger, healthier, and more empowered than I was before we started.

It comes from the sacred magic that happens whenever a roomful of people gather who, no matter what the marquee reads, are there because all of us in that room love

God and want to feel even closer to Him than we already are.

And last but not least, it comes from the luxury of knowing that when it's "just us," without cameras and lights and FCC regulations and censors and sponsors and commercial breaks, I can talk about whatever I damn well please.

The chapters in this little book were chosen from among the topics I enjoy discussing on my lecture tour, along with some of my favorite exercises and affirmations. I frankly believe that offering you ideas to think about and talk to your friends and loved ones about is only half of what I'm here for. If I don't offer you things to do with those ideas, I've cheated you and myself. I believe that *faith, love, hope,* and *spirituality* are really verbs, not nouns. They don't mean anything if they're not active, if they remain internal without ever affecting the way you treat the world in general, those spirits whose lives you touch every day, and most of all yourself and the sacred flame of God that burns inside you, your birthright from your divine Creator.

I hope these pages will give you something you need most right now, whether it's comfort, or a smile, or a new approach to an old problem, or just a good excuse to disappear for a few minutes to a quiet place that has nothing to do with wrapping paper, shopping, presents, a lack of presents, piped-in carols, forced merriment, and arguments about the best way to cook yams.

Until our travels cause our paths to cross, I love you, I thank you for this rich life you've given me, and I wish you the constant awareness of how deeply and eternally God treasures you.

SYLVIA C. BROWNE

The Exercises

Throughout this book you'll find passages in italics, which designate exercises I've found helpful on the issues each chapter deals with. Some of them are simple tips, but most of them can best be described as "meditations."

I'm a little hesitant to use the word *meditations,* actually. There are many people who are very skilled at traditional, classical meditation techniques and love the rituals involved, and I respect them for it. Sadly, though, a lot of well-publicized aspiring gurus and wanna-be "spiritual leaders" have made meditating sound like such a complicated, time-consuming process that it's not even worth trying for those of us who work for a living. So let me dispel a few myths about meditation in case you're as skeptical about it as you've been given reason to be.

- There's no shopping required. You don't need a special mat or rug. You don't need flowing robes, a leotard, or finger cymbals. You don't need a stack of CDs of flute, harp, or sitar music or Gregorian chants, unless you want them. You don't need incense or exotic herbs to burn. Candles are nice, and I love them for their calming atmosphere, but you don't need those either. All you need for a successful meditation is *you.*

- You don't have to be double-jointed in order to meditate. The famous lotus position is lovely if it's easy and natural for you, but nothing can stop a meditation more abruptly than muscle cramps. You don't have to sit on the floor if you don't feel like it either. I've seen people give up on meditating before they've even started because all they can think about is how physically uncomfortable they are. And you can form little Os with your thumbs and forefingers if you want, but why, if that means nothing to you?

- You definitely don't have to follow that often-quoted instruction to "let your mind go completely blank." Are they kidding? If you're like me, being told to let your mind go completely blank is a sure way to let your mind fill right up with everything from whether or not you need to stop for gas on the way home to whether or not you're the only person in the room who's a failure at letting their mind go completely blank. Nor do you have to "pick a spot on the wall to focus on until your eyes are fixed on nothingness." I tried that time and time again when I was first studying meditation techniques, and all my eyes ever fixed on was either how slightly crooked a picture on that wall was hanging or how much the wall itself could use a new coat of paint.

- You don't need to set aside an evening, or even an hour, to have a wonderful meditation experience. Take as much or as little quiet time as you can find for yourself, and never believe that if it doesn't take very long, it doesn't count.

So please rid your mind of any preconceived expectations of yourself or of the process of meditation. All it requires is your ability to visualize. If you think that's something you're not good at, pause right now and see if you can mentally trace the route you usually drive from your house to work, to the grocery store, to your favorite restaurant, or to your best friend's house. If you can do that, you're absolutely good enough at visualizing to give the exercises in this book a worthwhile try. It really is that simple.

What I'm about to describe is the method I've found the easiest and most comfortable to prepare for the exercises or meditations. As you proceed with the preparation, don't worry if there are parts in which you think you're just going through motions without feeling what you "should be" feeling. There is no "should be" here. There is no "wrong," and there's certainly nothing wrong with you. You'll feel what you feel, and you'll probably feel something different every time. There will be times when your conscious mind is hearing words without absorbing them. Again, there's nothing wrong, and there's no need to stop and give up. Your spirit mind, alive and well in your subconscious, isn't just absorbing the words, it's jumping for joy at this sign that you're acknowledging it and getting ready to take it for a beautiful, nourishing ride.

To make the exercises even easier, you might want to make an audiotape of the preparation below and then just add the meditations you'll find throughout the book. All I ask is that you do whatever it takes to make this experience relaxed, relaxing, comfortable, and above all, *yours.*

Remember, prayer is asking God, and meditation is listening for the answer. So just relax, close your eyes, and enjoy listening.

Sit in a comfortable chair with your feet flat on the floor and your spine resting against the chair's back. Loosen any tight clothing, and remove your shoes if you'll feel more relaxed without them. Place your hands lightly on your thighs with the palms facing upward, symbolically open and ready to receive God's grace and wisdom.

Picture a brilliant white warming glow

forming around you, flowing over you like a powerful, living, pulsating aura. This is the white light of the Holy Spirit, absorbing and destroying any negativity and darkness you've been carrying. This sacred white light is your constant protection, always available to you and there for the asking.

Now, close your eyes and take a long, deep breath, your cue to your body to begin relaxing. Slowly start breathing regularly and rhythmically as if you were going to sleep, and during that, silently ask that your intellect and emotion be cemented together for the journey you're about to take so that it stays in your mind and heart in the days and weeks ahead.

I want you to become conscious of the bottoms of your feet against the floor. Focus there until you're fully aware of them, as if for that moment they're the most important part of your body. Still breathing, regular, rhythmic, in no hurry, feel the bottoms of your feet begin to relax, every tight muscle in them unwinding, almost melting, until those muscles feel like strands of silk.

Using that same focus-and-relax process, slowly move that same glorious, relieving sense of spun silk to your ankles, into your calves, your knees, your thighs. Silently tell yourself, With every breath I feel my stress dissolve, and in its place I feel the energy and the healing and the power of my spirit taking over.

Keep moving your wonderful relaxation on up your body, through the pelvis, the reproductive organs, the intestines, on up to the trunk of your body and every organ, vein, artery, muscle, and tendon inside. All the way up to the neck and down the shoulders, calming, relieving, quieting, healing. Down the shoulders, into the upper arms, the lower arms, the hands, each finger, one at a time, completely relaxed, stress dissolving, replaced with energy and your spirit's divine power.

Move on to your face. Your mouth relaxes, your cheeks, the muscles of your jaw, on up to your nose and your closed eyes, the brows, the lids, where so much of your stress shows itself and where it is banished now, now that you, your own control, your own spirit, is in charge. No more anxiety, no more fear, no more negativity.

You are peaceful now, relaxed, relieved, healthy, strong, open, and eager. The white light of the Holy Spirit around you glows more brightly. You're ready to hear God's answers, ready for the exercises that will set your spirit free to listen and to fly unafraid for visits to these glimpses of its sacred eternity.

THE AFFIRMATIONS

Each chapter ends with an affirmation. If that word is unfamiliar to you, it simply means a positive, nurturing, truthful message from you to the God-center inside you. Repeat these affirmations once or as often as you like, silently or out loud, alone in your bathroom or car or at work or shopping or at a party, any time you want to remind yourself that you will tolerate no negativity, disrespect, or lack of integrity from yourself or anyone else, because, as a direct descendant of God Himself, you are nothing less than divine.

1

Grief

I've been asked more than once, "Sylvia, if you're so convinced that we never die, and you can see and hear spirits on The Other Side, why would you of all people grieve?" The answer is "Because I'm selfish, I'm human, and I'm *here.*"

Grief is the ultimate pain, the most hollow, numbing, paralyzing, hopeless, helpless aching on earth. It is a lone leaf blowing lost and futile in an empty doorway, an irreversible finality. When we're in its cruel grip, we would give anything—*anything*—to make it go away, to have everything back the way it was before this darkness came, when we had problems we could fix and options that we had some say in, if we could only remember what it was like to feel something besides such a stunning, overwhelming void.

I've been there. So have you. So has everyone on earth, which makes it even harder to imagine why we're not more universally compassionate toward each other. In fact, part of the unique depth of grief is its awful familiarity, because the truth is, it's an inevitable sorrow in our spirit from the moment we enter the womb.

Arriving in Grief

With the rare exception of those who only choose to spend one lifetime here, our spirits make the round-trip from The Other Side to earth over and over again in the course of eternity, at our own insistence, in pursuit of our greatest spiritual potential and service to God. Our lives at Home are busy, stimulating, euphoric, surrounded by exquisite beauty, friends, soul mates, Angels, and messiahs, thriving in God's awesome, palpable presence. It takes courage and enormous commitment for us to decide we need the tough challenges only life on earth can

provide, and to leave a paradise of unconditional love for this place where lasting love
of any kind is a scarce commodity. On The
Other Side, we understand that eternity
eliminates the concept of time altogether,
and when we leave Home we know we'll be
back again in the blink of an eye. But here,
where we measure our lives by linear days,
weeks, months, and years, that "blink of an
eye" seems like an eternity itself or, in our
darkest nights, that awful word *never.*

So when our spirits arrive in the womb
for another temporary leave of absence
from The Other Side, even though it's exactly what we chose to do for our own important purposes, we lose our sense of
timelessness and are born grieving our per-
ceived separation from our loved ones at
Home, just as we grieve on earth at our per-
ceived separation from a loved one who's
gone Home again. In a way, then, we're born
grieving, and part of the profound impact
that emotion has on us when we reexperi-
ence it during our lifetimes is its deeply
resonating familiarity from the moment of
birth. I promise there are babies all over the
world right this second who are looking
around at all these strangers making idiot

faces at them, having fleeting recall of those adored, adoring spirits they just said good-bye to on The Other Side, and wondering, *What the hell was I thinking?!* No wonder the first thing we do when we leave the womb is burst into tears.

The Grief Continues

One of the most distraught clients who ever sat in my office had had her life turned upside down in less than a week. On a Tuesday morning she'd been fired from a high-profile job she'd been devoted to for more than a decade, so that the company's new owner could replace her with his brother-in-law. The following Saturday her husband of sixteen years packed his bags and left her for her best friend. She wasn't there for me to tell her what her well-meaning friends had been assuring her, that her husband was a shallow opportunist whose love for her was solely dependent on her considerable career prestige. (It was true, but this was no time to tell her that.) She wasn't there for me to assure her that the affair between her husband and her best friend wouldn't last. (Also true, by the way. Her husband was cheating on her best friend within a year and begging my client two years later to take him back. She firmly and easily responded, "Thanks, but no thanks.") And she wasn't there for me to confirm that her career wouldn't just survive this outrage, it would flourish, although that was true as well. She was there to ask for my help in her emotional recovery from these two life-altering shocks. It had been several months and she felt she shouldn't still be feeling as devastated as she was. This was years ago and I can still hear her saying, "I should be doing better than this by now, Sylvia. After all, it's not as if somebody died."

She was a perfect example of the fact that very deep, very legitimate grief in our lives isn't just limited to the death of a loved one, and we do ourselves and each other an injustice when we fail to recognize it so that we can ask for or offer the special support grief demands. A broken relationship, a home destroyed either physically or emotionally, the termination of a valued or needed job, betrayal by someone we trusted, children "leaving the nest" or a dear friend moving far away, a separation or divorce, a major financial setback, an unwanted relocation—any loss of someone or something enormously important to us that severely alters the structure and security of our lives can trigger grief every bit as real as death.

I'm not talking about those drama addicts we've all known, who demand attention by "grieving" over everything from a flat tire to an overcooked meal, as if they equate their importance in this world with the exaggerated importance of their emotions. Trivializing grief does as great a disservice to humankind as being reluctant to recognize it. I'm talking about having the compassion to respect the enormity of grief when it hits us or someone close to us, whether or not there's an actual death involved, and act accordingly.

When a Loved One Is Grieving

A loved one's grief is a hard thing to deal with, let's face it. It can be more difficult to watch someone else's pain than to go through pain ourselves, because at least when it's our pain we can make decisions about it, tackle it, not tackle it, and feel some sense of control, even if it's minimal.

But sooner or later, unless we're hermits or cowards, we're likely to be faced with a grieving loved one and have that helpless, horrible feeling of not knowing what to do. I call what they're going through "the dark horse of grief." I call what they need from us "riding that horse right along with them." There are sensitive ways and insensitive ways to do that, a kind of "grief etiquette," for lack of a better term, that are worth remembering and following as best you can.

- A person in grief is a person who's in pure survival mode. Breathing, eating, and sleeping may be about the best they can do for a while. Taking care of the basics for them without their having to ask—grocery shopping, tidying up, doing their laundry, whatever you can manage without making a pest of yourself—can make an enormous difference until they care enough to start wanting to do those things for themselves again.
- Don't decide what their emotional needs should or shouldn't be at any given moment. Take your cues from them. Listen when they want to talk, be quiet with them when they don't, hold

them when they want to be held, and give them their privacy when they think that somehow solitude might make the pain more bearable. "It will help you to talk about it" or "It will do you good to get out and see people again" may be absolutely true for some people and completely wrong for others. But it's their decision to make, not yours, and you can help most by being available to support what *they* feel they need.

- Don't try to make them feel better by minimizing their loss. This is not the time to remind them of all their former complaints and frustrations about the person/pet/relationship/house/job they've lost. That amounts to expecting them to go from searing pain to "You're right, good riddance!" on cue, and if they're able to do that, they genuinely need psychiatric help. Grief is a process, not just a temporary state of mind, and everyone has to work through that process in their own way in their own time.

- Similarly, don't try to offer misguided perspective by topping your loved one's grief story with one of your own.

As I've discussed often at lectures and in other books, I lost nine people close to me in just three short months a few years ago, including, most horribly, my daddy, whom I adored. I was so numb with shock and sheer anguish that I barely remember much of anything from that dark, awful time. But I do remember a strange woman coming up to me at Daddy's memorial service, patting me on the back, and clucking, "This is nothing, dear. I once lost both my parents and my only brother all in one bus accident." I also remember wishing I had enough energy to strangle her. I'm sure her point was that if she could survive what she'd been through, I could survive too. But even if it's just a figure of speech, no one who's emotionally devastated appreciates hearing it's "nothing," or the popular and equally ignorant alternative, "You think *this* is bad . . . !"

- Proximity to grief can trigger some very odd reactions in us. On top of how hard it is to see someone we love in pain, we're either consciously or unconsciously aware of that grief we were born with and the grief we're likely to go through again, so the dread of "Next time it could be my turn" is both natural and scary. If you can rise above that natural dread and lend your support, in the hope that people will do the same for you when your turn *does* come, great. But if you can't, if their grief causes you enough discomfort, sadness, or panic that you can't contain it in front of them, make some gesture to let them know your thoughts are with them, but then stay away. There are few worse things you can do to a loved one than put them in the position of having to comfort you through their anguish.

- If you suspect that your loved one might want or need some trained help with what they're going through—a minister, a rabbi, a counselor, a medical doctor, a psychologist, a psychiatrist, a support group—track down and talk to some viable candidates for them before you even broach the subject. Again, you're dealing with someone who's in pure survival mode, who's performing even the most basic functions purely by rote. Suggesting, "You should find someone objective to talk to," is likely to sound as overwhelming to them as suggesting, "It's such a nice afternoon, why don't you run out and scale Mount Everest?" On the other hand, saying, "Here are the names and numbers of some people who'd love to help if you need them," makes it much easier for them to pick up the phone. Then let it be their decision, not yours. Take it from someone who's been working with grieving clients for almost half a century, it's okay if they're reluctant or skeptical and if you need to hold them by the hand to get them there, but ultimately they can only get meaningful help if they take the first step across the threshold by their own choice.

There's no question, riding the dark horse of grief with someone you love isn't easy. But sadly, it's a challenge you're almost guaranteed to face in this lifetime. And even more sadly, it's just as likely that you're going to *be* that grieving loved one sooner or later, and anyone who's been through it will agree with me, I'm sure, that it's the hardest challenge of all.

Surviving Your Own Grief

As I mentioned earlier, there are those who find it odd that I grieve at all, since I should be spiritual enough and psychic enough to know better. Does my grief mean I privately question the reality of The Other Side and the eternal lives of our spirits? Absolutely not. I don't just believe, I *know* those are simple, sacred truths. Even at my most decimated, my devout spirituality never waivers for an instant. As for my psychic gifts, yes, it is a fact that I have seen and heard thousands upon thousands of spirits and Angels in my lifetime, and that will continue until the day I go Home and live among them again. I've made countless astral trips to The Other Side and helped countless clients travel there as well, so I can guarantee that it's as real as, or even more real than, this earth we're visiting now.

Make no mistake about it, when I grieve, there's not a moment when I'm grieving for the loved one I've lost. I'm grieving for *me.* I'm grieving because I miss Daddy and my Grandma Ada and my dear friends, and I'm selfish enough to want them here with me, despite all the undeniable proof I have that they're still alive.

Even though only three short feet separate us from Home, as we discuss in the chapter on "Contacting The Other Side," earth and Home are two different dimensions with two different vibrational levels, theirs much higher than ours. Like most psychics and mediums, I was born with the ability to perceive that higher vibration. I can see and hear spirits on other levels, both ghosts who have left our level but haven't completed their transition to The Other Side yet and the many more transcended spirits who have. I've never kept count, but I can safely guess that I've seen and communicated with hundreds of thousands of them in my sixty-four years of this lifetime, as well as thousands of "normal" clients who have had encounters with spirits on those other levels.

If grieving were really limited to worrying about whether or not our loved ones are still alive and happy, I would cheer at every funeral. It's the practical difference between the two dimensions that causes me to grieve. The spirits I see are not these dense, gravity-bound bodies we live in while we're on earth, and their voices are quick bursts of high chirping words, distorted by the transition from one vibrational pitch to another. I'm blessed that I've seen and heard Daddy many times since he went Home. I cherish the signals he sends me, from the occasional unmistakable whiff of his beloved cherry-blend pipe tobacco to his well-timed playing of the music box he gave me, which won't make a sound on its own since I haven't wound it in at least twenty years. But I'd be lying if I said any of that is even a pale substitute for my yearning to have him walk into this room right now, put his strong arms around me, and, in his smooth baritone voice, make me laugh as no one else could but him. It's selfish and ungrateful of me, but the truth is, I grieve because he's on The Other Side, having a great time, happy and healthy and not even missing me because as far as he's concerned, I'll be there with him in another minute or two, while I'm stuck here living out my own chart, trying to make the most of the thirty long years I have left until he and I are living fulltime on the same dimension again.

It always fascinates me that when I'm writing, it's as if my clients find out somehow and gang up to bring me relevant contributions, no matter which subject I happen to be working on at the time. During this particular chapter, I talked to two separate grieving families with beautiful stories to share, all the more touching because these people didn't consider themselves extraordinary, and because both stories involved children.

You may have met William and his daughter Amy right along with me, at a taping of *The Montel Williams Show.* When Amy and her twin sister were three years old, the sister was diagnosed with a brain tumor. She died at the age of six, and Amy, now a young adult, has been visited by and seen the spirit of her beloved twin ever since. Almost more amazing to me, since it's a comparatively rare experience, was what William had witnessed. He was a sweet, soft-spoken, modest man, certainly not someone so eager for attention that he'd make up a good story to get himself on television. He was afraid I'd think he was crazy, as if I'm in a position to think *anyone* is crazy. But William was alone with Amy's six-year-old twin, a foot or two from her hospital bed, at the moment she "died," and he was blessed to actually witness her spirit, an unmistakable mist, leaving her body. I remember his saying that when he looked back at her body again, he knew it was vacant, it was just the vehicle she'd occupied during her brief stay on earth. He didn't need me to confirm that he hadn't imagined it and that that's exactly what he had seen. In fact, he wasn't asking. He was just a lovely man who wanted me and the audience to hear the exquisite news that he hadn't seen his child die at all. With his own eyes, he'd really seen his child live. Fifteen years later, his voice was still a mixture of joy and sorrow as he told me about it. But sorrow for her, after that quiet miracle? Not a chance.

I was also very touched by Alexis, a quietly elegant client in her early thirties. Her four-year-old son Ethan had passed on only a few weeks before I met her, after a brave battle with leukemia. In his last moments on earth he'd looked up at her with absolute peace and said, "I'm going to die, Mama. It's okay. I promised God." At Ethan's funeral, Alexis was sitting in numb shock, wondering how and if she could survive without this child who had given her life such love and purpose, when she unmistakably heard his voice, whispering in her ear, strong and playful, "Mama, I'm going to kiss you on the nose," followed by a tiny, gentle breath of cool air on the bridge of her nose, exactly where the two of them made a private habit of kissing each other good-night. It was so real it made her gasp, and she found herself smiling, filled with a rush of joy. Her friends and even her minister listened patiently and compassionately when she shared this wonderful moment with them later, and then one by one they assured her that grief can create all sorts of hallucinations, but if it brought her comfort to think it was real, there was probably no harm in it. "Sylvia, I was in a lot of pain," she told me, "but I wasn't far enough gone to hallucinate. It happened. Ethan talked to me and kissed me on the nose at his funeral. What I can't understand is, my friends and my minister claim to believe in life after death. Ethan gave me proof that life after death is real. So how can these people turn around and insist I only imagined a sign that what they believe is true?"

It's a question I've asked myself a million times. Why believe in something as joyful as the fact that our spirits have eternal life, but promptly scoff at all the proof around us that we're right? Grief is excruciating enough as we face the rest of our lives without the human presence of our deceased loved ones. If I didn't know with absolute certainty that our loved ones are still as alive as we are—actually *more* alive—and that they're around us all the time, I would just crawl into a corner, curl up in a ball, and never come out again.

Another question that comes up often that I *can* answer, though, which both of those clients' stories remind me of, is "Why did God allow this innocent child (or this good person) to die?" That's easy. He didn't! A God of perfect, eternal, unconditional love doesn't suddenly turn mean, vengeful, and sadistic, and just swoop down and take us against our will as some kind of cruel hobby. No, like everything else in our lives, as we'll discuss in the chapter "Charting Our Life's Purpose," *we* make that choice. Yes, even children, whose spirits are as ageless and fully developed as ours on The Other Side— we *all* chart the timing and the circumstances of our trip Home before we come here.

So please, *please,* when you're facing the

utter despair of losing a loved one, don't add to your grief by worrying about their well-being. My book *Life on The Other Side* can offer you a detailed description of where they are and what they're doing, but the bottom line is that, like everyone else at Home, they're happy, they're in perfect health, they're busy, they're surrounded by countless friends from many lives, they love you completely and unconditionally, if there were any hard feelings between you they're completely forgotten and understood, they visit you often whether you feel them or not, and as far as they're concerned the two of you will be together again in no time at all and they're probably already planning the party for your reunion. Whatever part of your grief is about them, I promise it's safe to let it go and limit your pain to how terribly you miss them.

And by the way, there's an old wives' tale that when we grieve, we bind our loved one's spirit to earth and keep it from transcending to its rightful place on The Other Side. Believe me when I tell you that's not true, but I can tell you where it came from. For one thing, as I also describe in *Life on The Other Side,* our loved ones go through several different orientation processes when they first arrive back Home, so in many cases they're temporarily unavailable until they've finished their orientation. For another thing, one of the many awful effects of grief is that it throws us into such a numb state of sorrow that we're often blocked from any ability we might have to sense visits from our loved ones until we're starting to heal and recover. I saw my cherished Grandma Ada almost immediately after she died, but it took Daddy eight months to show up. And knowing me as he did, it didn't surprise him one bit when I greeted him with a relieved but impatient "What the hell took you so long?!" So don't let it throw you if you don't notice signs from your loved one right away. They have their orientation to deal with, you have your grief to deal with, but it's a guarantee that sooner or later they'll be with you again, and all you have to do is keep an open mind and pay attention.

Getting Through It

I wish that, as was with all the other chapters in this book, I had some wonderful exercise to help lessen your grief, or to speed you through it when you're in its grip. Unfortunately, learning to survive it is part of the reason we chose to experience another life on earth, since it's absolutely true that what doesn't kill us makes us stronger. Grief ultimately strengthens and expands our spirits, however small and powerless it makes us feel at the time. There is no grief on The Other Side, so this is the only place where we can confront it, grow from it, and add its depth to our eternal wisdom. Remember, our time on earth is school. Grief is the toughest course we sign up for. To pass that course, we have to survive it, it's as simple and as hard as that, and here are a few tips that I hope can help you through it:

- As I mentioned earlier, grief, whether it's a loved one's or your own, puts you in a survival mode. Nothing more, nothing less. Normal life seems like an alien concept. You can't remember what "normal" felt like, and you certainly can't believe it's something you can ever look forward to again. As basic as these reminders are, be sure to eat and sleep as regularly as you can, because in survival mode, basics become all the more important and yet the easiest to disregard when you truly believe that nothing, including your own maintenance, seems worth the effort it takes. And then, just hang on. You *will* be back to normal again someday. It won't be the same, and I won't give you the false hope of telling you it will. But one day in the near or distant future, you'll wake up one morning with some purpose and some form of peace in whatever your new definition of "normal" turns out to be.

- Ask for any and all help you need. Those who truly love you want to help if you can give them even a hint of what they can do, and there are doctors, psychologists, and support groups who really do understand exactly what you're going through and are trained to make a difference. Take advantage of your standing invitation to call the crisis hotline at my office, any time of day or night, at (408) 379-7070. No one can take your pain away, but there are people out there who can and want to take your hand and guide you through it, so that someday you'll be strong enough to do the same for someone else.

- This is just a fact, no matter how tempting it might be to fool yourself about it: Drugs and alcohol can't take your pain away, either, they can only postpone it. Hard as it is, with the exception of prescribed medication from a qualified physician, don't anesthetize your grief. Feel it, endure it, and get it over with. Artificially putting it off gives grief the power to jump out and take you down when you least expect it, and an emotion that strong, hidden in denial and buried in the body, is guaranteed to take a horrifying toll on your physical health if you don't let yourself fully experience it at the time it hits.

- Every single day, put out the most effort you can possibly muster. Don't wait until you "feel like it," because very probably you're not going to "feel like it" for quite a while. The truth is, the more you can gently push yourself, the more quickly your healing is likely to begin. I recommend going back to work as soon as possible. If work is too much to handle, settle for something as basic as getting out of bed and getting dressed. There will be mornings when even that will seem like an overwhelming, pointless chore. But it will send a message to your body that you're still alive and functioning, and your mind will catch up with that message when it can.

- Be more selective than you've ever been about who and what is around you. Even the most subtle negativity is unacceptable now, from people, reading material, television, or anything else in your environment. This is the time to take the loud and clear position "Be supportive or stay away from me."

- Embrace everyone and everything that is positive, supportive, and spiritually nourishing. Read every word of comfort you can find, and ask your friends to pray for you and with you. Don't be discouraged if you feel as if it's not doing any good or making any immediate difference. One extraordinary fact about grief that you'll only discover when you're emerging from its darkness is that it truly does expand the soul. Your capacity to give and accept love deepens as you heal. You absorb more hope, comfort, and truth about your divine, eternal connection to God than you'll probably recognize while you're grieving, but the day will come when you look back and marvel at how much closer you've grown to Him just from the sheer strength it took to survive this unspeakable pain.

- Hard as it is to believe, whatever event triggered your grief is an event you charted to confront before you came here. The rest of that thought *isn't* "So stop complaining, you asked for this." The rest of that thought *is* the very important point that in the larger view of your life and the lives of those you're sharing it with, there was and is a greater purpose to this loss than you can possibly see from the temporary abyss of your grief, so hang on—precisely because you charted it, there is a result around the corner that you'll definitely want to be around to witness. Such clichés as "Sooner or later, some good will come from this" and "One way or another these things always work out for the best" are, without realizing it, another way of saying, "Since this is a part of the contract I made with God, there's a reason for it that I'll understand and appreciate someday."

- Finally, if there's anything you feel was left unsaid and undone between you and the loved one who's gone, say it and do it now. I swear to you from the bottom of my heart that they're around you, they'll hear you, and they're watching over you and loving you with the infinite understanding of The Other Side until the day you step into their arms as they joyfully welcome you Home.

THE AFFIRMATION

"Dearest Mother and Father God,

"My despair feels like a tangible force, so engulfing that it encompasses my thoughts and my heart. Knowing and accepting this, I ask You to help me ride it through and emerge from it brighter, stronger, more loving, and more loved than ever before.

"I realize that reaching the depths of my soul's sorrow is a ferocious lesson. But I have faith that, armed with the power of

Your mighty golden sword of pure, infinite, perfect love, I will triumph over my pain, loss, and suffering and finally find Your light waiting to guide me through this vast, dark desert. Amen."

2

Discovering Life's Purpose

Before we leave The Other Side for another lifetime on earth, we compose an incredibly detailed chart of every aspect of our upcoming incarnation. If you look at some aspects of your life and think, *Are you saying I chose this? Not a chance!* I know exactly how you feel. Sometimes I'm sure I must have been either drunk or insane when I wrote my chart. But, yes, that is what I'm saying, and it's really a logical and very comforting fact in God's gorgeous, eternal plan for all of us.

There are a few rare, extraordinary souls who only incarnate once and then choose to do the rest of their work and their learning at Home. One divine example is Jesus

Christ, whose awareness of His chart is recorded throughout the beginning of the New Testament. Alone in the garden of Gethsemane, knowing His disciple Judas had betrayed Him to the Roman soldiers and that He would be captured and crucified, Jesus even prayed to be released from the contract He'd written, with a human and frightened "Father, if thou art willing, remove this cup from me." (Luke 22:42) Then, surrendering Himself to His destiny in God's sacred plan for Him, He finished the prayer with "Nevertheless not my will, but thine, be done." Jesus even knew it was written in His chart that His beloved disciple Peter would disclaim knowing Him when the crowds had turned against Him. "I tell you, Peter, the cock will not crow this day, until you three times deny that you know me." (Luke 22:34) And after Jesus was captured, Peter did deny knowing Him, and on the third denial, "while he was still speaking, the cock crowed. And the Lord turned and looked at Peter. And Peter remembered the word of the Lord . . . and he went out and wept bitterly." (Luke 22:60–62)

To say that Jesus is the exception to almost every human rule is a gross understatement. Like all of us, though, He did write a detailed chart, a life's purpose, before He came here, that He knew He had to fulfill, despite a moment of understandable weakness. Neither Jesus nor any of the other great disciples whose presence has graced this world will ever need another incarnation on earth to accomplish all they intended, and please run screaming from anyone who claims to be the second coming of any of them.

But the vast majority of us, more flawed but no less cherished by God, live many lifetimes here, by our own choice, to learn specific lessons for the ongoing progress of our spirits by experiencing the negativity only this boot camp called earth can provide. Our spirits arrive here with the knowledge we've gained from every previous lifetime and from our vast studies on The Other Side, and our goals for each new life are based on what we believe we still need to work on. Arriving on earth without a chart meticulously designed to achieve those goals would be no different than showing up for the first day of college with no clue where we're going to live, what classes we're going to take, what subjects we're interested or not interested in, where our talents lie, or even what kinds of people we might want to make friends with or avoid.

And how wonderful, how infinitely loving of God, not to let us come here without a detailed plan, not to just send us wandering around this rough place at random trying to run into as few walls as possible. Even *with* a plan, from time to time I think we all feel as if that's what we're doing anyway. But not only do we compose our chart on The Other Side, with the help of our Spirit Guide and a team of other brilliantly trained souls who are far wiser than we are, but we also are guaranteed to reach the goals in that chart before we head Home again. The question is whether we'll reach them the easy way or the hard way. And that's the reason our chart doesn't mean there is no such thing as free will.

Let's say each of us comes to earth with the goal of getting to the North Pole in this lifetime, and we all start in Alaska. Look around at the people you know, or even at yourself. I promise, you can easily spot those who, with that goal in mind, immediately headed south, or started off with no map wearing nothing but a light jacket and complaining every step of the way, or never got more than five miles from home before they'd have to turn around and go back because they forgot something. But you've also seen those rare few who, thoroughly prepared, with map in hand, stride confidently north, accepting the cold and hunger and exhaustion and bitter wind as inevitable parts of the trip, not to be victimized by the journey but to survive it.

Free will allows us to choose the ease or the difficulty, the grace or the resentment, the passion or the laziness, the care or the neglect with which we'll follow our chart. If we chart a cut on the arm when we're nineteen years old, we can clean it, bandage it, and help it heal, or we can ignore it and let it develop into a serious, potentially threatening infection. A charted car accident can be a fender-bender or a near-fatal disaster. A charted marriage can be invested in or abused. So please don't get the impression that the chart eliminates options, negates free will, and suggests that some sort of inescapable fatalism is ruling our lives. Not only does it leave us with plenty of options as we go along, but don't forget, our charts aren't dictated to us by some great cosmic committee. *We* compose them, on The Other Side, after *we've* made the choice to experience another life on earth, which means that free will is an essential part of the process from the very beginning.

When I say the chart is detailed, it's an understatement. We chart our parents, our place and date and time of birth, our race, our sexual preference, our physical and physiological strengths and weaknesses, our siblings, our children, our friends, our enemies, our love relationships both good and bad, our financial status, our interests, our disinterests, our mental capacity, our advantages, our hurdles, every tiny aspect of our lives, all specifically chosen based on what we've already experienced in past lives and our interim time on The Other Side and what we're determined to accomplish in this life.

But we also make decisions about some crucial broadstrokes of our lives. If the details of the chart are individual measures of music, these broadstrokes are the verses, the chorus, and the movements of the song itself. Understanding them can help us understand that the forces and conflicts we're faced with aren't random at all. We designed them, to guarantee that our time here won't be wasted, and that this tough school we're all attending will have the greatest possible impact on the eternal journey of our soul.

Life Themes

I've done tens of thousands of past-life regressions for clients over the years, and every single time I ask a client who's reliving a previous incarnation, "What is your purpose in this life?" they have an immediate one-word answer. I began keeping track of those answers decades ago, and through an enormous amount of further research, I discovered that when we compose our charts on The Other Side, we choose a primary and secondary life theme for ourselves to help focus our goals for our upcoming lives.

There are forty-four life themes in all, ranging from Activator to Winner. I've listed and described them in detail in my books *The Other Side and Back* and *Life on The Other Side,* so it would be redundant to repeat them all here. But our primary life theme is our innermost motivation, the engine that drives our spirit, while our secondary life theme is the underlying force we have to pull against to keep ourselves on track.

I'm a glaring example of the typical conflict between a primary theme and a secondary theme. My primary theme is Humanitarian. That's what compels me and lies at the core of everything I do, and my psychic gifts and my church are simply two of the tools I use to accomplish that theme. But my secondary theme is Loner. Left to my own devices, without the Humanitarian commitment I made before I came here, I'd be happily and selfishly sitting by myself under a tree somewhere in Kenya, reading, writing, and going days at a time without the sound of another human voice. Obviously, giving in to my secondary theme would defeat my primary theme, so even though it's a constant temptation, I know that it's a luxury I'll never be able to afford and that I chose it as a constant test of my passion for the real reason I'm here.

There's not always an apparent link between your primary theme and your chosen career. A man came to me recently who'd read my other books and was very curious to hear about his primary theme. He was more than a little skeptical when I told him he was a Healer. It seems he's been an auto mechanic all of his adult life and never had the slightest curiosity about, let alone the scholastic talent for, the fields of medicine or psychiatry. But the more we talked, the more he realized that he's always the first person his family and friends come to when they have a problem, he's nursed any number of stray and injured animals back to health, and he's the first to jump into the middle of arguments among his coworkers and help restore peace and order. As I assured him, there are countless gifted Healers in this world who've never seen a scalpel or had a framed college diploma hung on their wall, just as every other life theme is represented by people whose means of earning a living seem completely unrelated.

So as you try to figure out what your primary theme might be, don't look out at the surroundings of your workday. Look *in,* at the constant urge that echoes in your spirit no matter where your life might take you and dictates the impact you have on the people around you. And then, to discover your secondary theme, simply look for the force in your spirit that seems to be constantly whispering in your ear trying to tempt you toward less of a life than you know you're really here to live.

Option Lines

I was especially relieved to learn about option lines, because until then, I thought I was a chronic failure in one area of my life for no good reason, no matter how hard I tried. And after almost five decades of readings, I have yet to meet a client who doesn't feel exactly the same way. Now I know it's not just our imagination, there *is* one area of life we're each bound to struggle with more than any other, and furthermore, we're the geniuses who chose it.

When writing our charts on The Other Side, we're given a list of seven option lines to choose from: love, health, finance, career, spirituality, family, and social life. The option line we declare ours for the life we're about to live is essentially the area of this earthly school we've decided to major in, the area we'll agonize over the most, and the area in which we feel we have the most to learn.

My option line is family. So I guess it makes sense that while I chose a wonderful father and a grandmother I idolized, I also chose an abusive mother and a sister I'm still occasionally estranged from to this day. I've had four husbands. My two sons, whom I cherish, have two different fathers and have only recently reconciled (thank you, God!) after not speaking to each other for years. They've both been through their own rough times on the family front, believe me, while being brilliant fathers to my three treasured grandchildren. At any rate, some how, out of those raw materials, I've tried for sixty-four years to manufacture a sane, happy, Norman Rockwell family, all of us hand in hand, skipping merrily through life together behind our white picket fence. The contrast between my idealized image and the reality is, to put it mildly, jaw dropping. But because I know that this is the option line I chose, at least I understand why I can't seem to get this family thing right no matter how much love and effort I put into it, why my feelings about it are so passionate, and why it's so important for me in this lifetime to keep trying.

If you ever find yourself envying someone who appears to be so much luckier than you are or have so much more than you do, remember that *everyone* has an option line they struggle with, it's just that some people are better at hiding it than others. I have a celebrity client, brilliantly talented, universally admired, as smart and witty and charming as any man I've ever met, with a forty-year career anyone would be proud to claim. His option line? Finance. Between alimony, child support, a dishonest business manager, a gambling addiction he's still in treatment for, a long list of failed "surefire" investments, and a mistaken belief that his popularity has lasted so long that it's indestructible, he's now been unemployed for three years after a few unsuccessful movies in a row that he took only because he desperately needed the money, and he's praying the tabloids won't find out that he's filed for bankruptcy, as if his fraying career isn't humiliating him enough. There's a good chance you've thought of him as someone you'd happily trade places with in a heartbeat. The truth is, he would happily trade places with you. In fact, when I explained option lines to him, he wondered, only half kidding, if there were some way we could swap my "family" and his "finance."

I'm sure that if you do an honest scan of

your life, you'll recognize which of the seven option lines is yours. Figuring it out is worth the time it takes, if only to reassure yourself that you're not being victimized by some dark, random force, you're just struggling through that one subject you yourself selected to be the hardest for you this time around.

Exit Points

Full of love, joy, perfect health, and optimism as we are on The Other Side when we're composing our chart, we're very aware that this lifetime we're embarking on is going to be difficult at best, and we're smart enough to write in five separate exit points, or opportunities to head Home again when we feel we've accomplished all we intended when we came here. We can take advantage of any of those five exit points we choose as we go along—the first, which usually occurs when we're infants or very young children, the fifth, which is typically charted for our senior-citizen years, or any time in between.

The classic example of an exit point is surgery, illness, an accident on the road, a fall, a sports injury—any event that either is or could be life threatening. We've all heard of people who survived an accident or illness against all odds, which simply means they chose not to exercise that particular exit point. We've also heard of people who didn't survive a relatively minor accident, illness, or surgery, or, in other words, decided to take advantage of an exit point that might not have looked like an exit point to anyone else. While nothing is more devastating than the loss of a child, there can be a tiny particle of comfort in the knowledge that even infant bodies house timeless, ageless spirits who composed a chart before they came here and opted for the first exit point they themselves designed.

Some exit points are so subtle we might not think twice about them when they happen. We'll come upon a car wreck by the side of the road, for example, breathe a sigh of relief that we weren't in it, and maybe even pause for a moment to realize that we would have been in it if we'd been at that spot five minutes earlier. But rarely do we go further, as we should, and take a close look at what exactly kept us five short minutes from danger. Narrowly escaping or avoiding an exit point is the same as choosing not to exercise it as far as our charts are concerned, after all. So when you look back on your life and try to count your exit points to date, don't assume that if you've never been through a near-death trauma, you've never had an exit point.

At the same time, don't panic if you look back and realize you've had three or four exit points so far. That doesn't necessarily mean that your time may be almost up. I had my third and fourth exit points when I was in my forties. I'm now in my sixties, and I'm not heading Home until I'm in my nineties. When we write them in the first place, we coordinate their occurrences with the rest of our chart, rather than spacing them out or bunching them up on some kind of supposedly logical earthly schedule. The timing of every passing, every exit point taken, is perfect in relation to the chart it's a part of and the spirit who composed it, whether or not that perfection ever becomes apparent to the rest of us, until we're Home again, where we'll understand everything.

I was with a client a while ago, a dark-haired woman named Maria, who had lost her six-month-old baby to SIDS (sudden infant death syndrome) a year earlier and was still understandably grieving. When I explained exit points to her, she couldn't imagine why a newborn would feel it had accomplished the goals of its chart when its lifetime had barely started. But the longer we talked, the more we discovered together that the death of this innocent child had ultimately reignited the deep love and commitment between Maria and her husband that they had simply lost track of, and it also had brought a real closeness between Maria and her mother for the first time in Maria's life as they comforted each other. There are spirits like Maria's baby whose goals are selfless, who are here for the benefit of their family, or society, or the medical community, or the justice system, or certainly the recipient of an organ donation. And I was so happy to be able to give Maria some wonderful news before she left. She and her husband had recently started discussing having another baby: They will. A boy. The same spirit they lost a year ago, who will now be born into a strong, loving, fully committed marriage, with the world's second most adoring grandmother (anyone who tries for first place in that department will have to contend with me), and who will live a long, happy, and very healthy life.

There's one more essential thing to remember about exit points that I'll insist on stressing every time this subject comes up: Suicide is never, ever to be thought of, let alone used, as an exit point. No chart ever written has included suicide, and since our charts are our contracts with God, suicide represents the ultimate broken commitment. That's not to say that every suicide is evil, damned, and punished. Such circumstances as mental illness, or severe substance abuse to the point where someone truly has no idea what they're doing, or even certain extreme medical conditions, can't possibly be compared to suicides motivated by revenge, cruelty, or cowardice. But please, *please,* don't misinterpret the fact of exit points as an excuse to manufacture an exit point of your own by even considering taking your own life.

Following the Chart

Our charts aren't just composed in theory and stored in the memories of our spirit, our Spirit Guide, and God. They're quite real and tangible, written in gilt script on parchment scrolls and meticulously filed and cared for in a magnificent building on The Other Side called the Hall of Records. I've had the awesome experience of astrally visiting the Hall of Records many times, and a recent client who traveled there during hypnosis went through the same frustration on her trip as hundreds of other clients and I have gone through.

Her name was Helena, and she was a great hypnosis subject, skeptical but open minded, with no predisposed ideas of what might or might not happen during her regression and even warning me in advance that she wasn't about to pretend to be "under" or make things up just to make me feel better. I assured her that not only was that fine with me, I consider anything less than absolute honesty during any reading or regression to be a complete waste of my time and my clients' money.

Not all clients who revisit their past lives through hypnosis also revisit their time on The Other Side between lives. But after quickly and easily regressing to the life immediately before this one, when she was a blacksmith named Dwayne Rhodes in the early 1900s, Helena took an unmistakable trip to The Other Side, described the Hall of Records in precise detail, and then actually located the chart she knew she'd already written for the life she's living now. She took the scrolled chart from its shelf, excitedly unrolled it, and found it blank.

Just as my scroll for this life was blank when I found it in the Hall of Records, just as my clients' scrolls for this life are blank when they locate theirs.

My Spirit Guide, Francine, confirmed my conclusion from these many identical incidents—we're not allowed to see our own charts, we're supposed to *live* them, until the lifetimes they apply to are over.

I can read your chart. Every legitimate psychic can read your chart. That's how we can tell you what's coming up in your life, what to watch out for, what Mr. or Ms. Right looks like, how many children you'll have, etc., etc. But you'll hear me and every other legitimate psychic readily admit that we're not psychic about ourselves, and now you know why—our own charts are as off limits to us as yours are to you. I'm not sure if it's selfish or lazy or a little of both that I sometimes wish I could sneak glances at my chart from time to time, if only to scan a few personal situations I'm currently struggling with to see how they end, or at least see what I'm supposed to learn from them, since I'm the one who wrote them in the first place. But it's God's plan that we not read our charts until we're Home again, and one thing you'll never hear me do is try to second-guess Him.

So while I can't offer an exercise that will give you a peek at your chart to see whether or not you're on track, and how to get back on track if you're not, I can give you a list of guidelines that you should sit quietly and review at least every three months. They're only worthwhile if you're willing to address them with as much ego-free honesty as possible, and then to take action on what you discover.

Regardless of the details of your chart, your life themes, your option lines, and your exit points, the following guidelines apply to all of us:

- *None of us wrote a mistake-free chart. The purpose of our mistakes is to learn from them. We can't learn from them if we refuse to take responsibility for them, and when we shift the blame for our mistakes we deprive ourselves of knowledge, which is a guaranteed way to throw ourselves off the path of our chart. Think back on mistakes you've avoided admitting. Then do yourself and your spirit the honor of owning up to them, with courage and no excuses. The freedom you'll feel is actually the joy of stepping closer to your own chosen purpose.*

- *Again, think back on your mistakes and remember that you wrote them into your chart to learn from them. The sure way of knowing whether or not you've learned from mistakes is to take an honest look at whether or not you're repeating them. The bad news is, if you're repeating the same mistakes over and over again, you're off track. The good news is, it's never too late to declare a lesson learned and those mistakes a part of your past, not your future.*

- *Every chart is also designed for us to learn from and overcome negativity, which is why we left the perfect, nega-*

tivity-free paradise of The Other Side for this imperfect, negativity-ridden hell of earth. Learning from it means understanding how destructive negativity is, not only for this world and humankind but also for the progress of every spirit who's living here, including our own. Overcoming it doesn't just mean avoiding it as best we can. Overcoming it means confronting it, refusing to tolerate it or promote it, and doing active spiritual battle against it, and I guarantee your chart contains a promise to your soul and to God that during this lifetime you would do exactly that.

* *When we write our chart on The Other Side, we are thriving in the immediate presence of God and in full, joyful awareness of our God-center as His children. At the core of every chart is our determination to feel the same peaceful, powerful, blessed certainty of that God-center as we feel at Home, and to express it every day of our lives. Expressing our God-center means devoting regular time and energy to some kindness, some cause, some purpose,*

that's bigger and finer than we are, that elevates this earth and makes it better for our having been here. Praising God without taking every opportunity to extend ourselves to all of His children, which include every living being around us, cancels out the progress our spirit always intends.

- *And again, because every chart is designed to express the abiding awareness of our sacred God-center, no chart ever includes suicide, causing ourselves deliberate physical or emotional harm, or abandoning our self-respect. The life purpose inherent in every chart includes a promise to love ourselves, because by loving ourselves we declare our love for the Father who gave us life to begin with.*

THE AFFIRMATION

"I know that with each new lifetime I write a new chart that will further me along the path God and I mapped together, which will inevitably wind its way toward perfection. According to my chart, I will sometimes run, joyful and free, and I will sometimes fall, stand again, and learn from the pain. But I will always remember God's promise, that while step after step may be hard and halting, the whole of the journey will be my most divine reward."

3

Past Lives

One of my most comforting, affirming surprises has been the ongoing confirmation, beyond any doubt, that we live many lifetimes on this earth. Needless to say, the truth that we live life after life here isn't thrilling because it's such a rollicking, nonstop picnic. But the truth that we live life after life here *is* thrilling because it proves that in fearing death, we're really fearing something that doesn't even exist.

I would love to claim that in my infinite wisdom I was born aware of and fascinated by past lives. But, no, I was too preoccupied with other things, like my ongoing suspicion that instead of being psychic I was actually just nuts. I didn't believe or disbelieve in past lives, I simply didn't give the issue much thought one way or the other. Like so many other important answers, I had to trip over this one without even consciously asking the question.

Because it was such a pivotal event in my career and my life, I'll repeat a story I've often told, if only to underscore that when I say I tripped over my first encounter with past lives, I'm not just being modest. In my late teens I became a certified hypnotist, thinking it would be a great way to help people lose weight, stop smoking, and generally rid themselves of any other subconscious emotional habits and clutter from this life that might be getting in their way. I was in my office one day, working with yet another hypnotized client, this one with an insomnia problem, when he suddenly started babbling, in the present tense, about his hard life as a pyramid builder, and then lapsed into several minutes of the goofiest-sounding nonsense syllables I'd ever heard. I thought he was having a psychotic breakdown right before my eyes, and I was rethinking my staff's suggestion about having a panic button installed when, just as suddenly, he snapped out of it and reverted to the nice, sane, English-speaking man who'd entered my office an hour earlier.

I sent a tape of the session to a psychology-professor friend at Stanford, expecting him to agree with my suspicion that this poor client needed psychiatric help. Instead, he called back three days later, almost breathless with excitement, to tell me that after considerable research, he and his colleagues were in unanimous agreement that those goofy nonsense syllables were actually my client speaking fluent seventh-century-B.C. Assyrian, a language that would have been very popular among pyramid builders. Just to be thorough, I did call my client and asked if by any chance he happened to be a linguist, and/or fluent in ancient Assyrian. He was so overly polite when he said he wasn't that I'm still convinced he thought *I* was having a psychotic episode.

That incident was the trigger to my intensive exploration of the possibility of past lives. I began reading everything I could find on the subject and studying techniques to safely steer hypnosis clients to their previous incarnations without ever again letting them wander aimlessly among the pyramids while I sat there saying, "Duh." I thought it would be an interesting exercise for any clients who happened to have lived before. I had no idea that an even more important understanding was yet to come—that not only have we all had past lives, but also, in more ways than we consciously realize, *those past lives have an impact on our present lives every single day.*

Tens of thousands of past-life regressions and forty-plus years of research later, I know that we've all lived before, that we're all deeply affected by our previous lifetimes, and that the interaction of our multiple lives follows God's simple, perfect, logical plan for these souls He created.

Each of our spirits, distinctive and uniquely ours, was created by God an eternity ago, with an eternity left to live, learn, and grow, on an exquisite journey toward our greatest potential. Part of that journey is spent at Home on The Other Side, but we take occasional side trips to earth for the lessons we have to learn the hard way, and, believe me, it doesn't get harder than this. The events we call "birth" and "death" are nothing more than the means by which our spirits travel from one dimension to another.

Through it all, we're still that same unique spirit God created, gaining wisdom and blessed power along the way, and every step we take on our eternal journey is affected by every step and misstep it took to get there.

Here's a simple analogy. Think of our lifetimes on earth as a school year, and summer vacations as The Other Side. Isn't it silly to imagine that after every summer vacation, we'd show up for a new school year a completely different person, having had none of the benefit of classes and experiences from the year before, so that we're just perpetually starting from scratch on our first day every fall? We'd never get out of kindergarten if that were true, nor would we recognize any of our friends and classmates or, for that matter, ourselves. What possible progress could our spirits make, and how could our souls contain so much cumulative knowledge, if that described God's intention for us?

Instead, we're the same unique spirits throughout eternity, advancing our way through this tough school on earth and the blissful, sacred education at Home. We repeat courses we find more difficult. We ourselves decide when we're ready to tackle more advanced work on earth and then when we're ready to graduate and concentrate exclusively on our postgraduate studies on The Other Side. And never, ever, do we forfeit our history, our infinite wealth of experience, or the original identity that is our birthright from God.

Cell Memory

Because our spirits entered this life in possession of every moment that came before, we really are affected, physically and emotionally, by every past life we've lived, especially through a phenomenon known as "cell memory."

Every time the spirit leaves yet another of these amazing, complicated, gravity-challenged human bodies, it takes with it all the memories it experienced in that body, as well as the basic sense of what being in a body is like. If, after a few decades, centuries, or millennia on The Other Side, the spirit opts for another lifetime on earth and finds itself in a body again, it resonates with the familiarity of that sensation and, from its vantage point in the subconscious mind, sends its memories flooding into every living cell of that body. The cells respond to the past-life memories they've received from the spirit mind, and the result is that from birth until death, our conscious minds and bodies are constantly reacting not only to all the input from this life but also to all the spirit's messages to our cells based on everything it remembers about being in a body.

I've had so many fascinating encounters with cell memory that I could write a book on the subject. In fact, I'm sure I will. The joy in uncovering it and working with it is the remarkable ease with which it can permanently relieve a lot of present-day pain. It's as if a client under hypnosis almost can't wait to tell me about some thorn from some past life that's hurting them all over again now that cell memory has been activated, and I'm given the honor of removing that thorn so that they can start to heal.

One of my first experiences with the healing power of cell memory happened shortly after I'd learned the gentle skill of uncovering past lives through hypnosis while never leading a client or planting suggestions, to make sure all the information was coming from the client, not from me. Her name was

Leigh. She was thirty-five but looked older, a sad, tense woman who was fiercely clinging to an abusive marriage. Against all logic and her own obvious intelligence, she was so busy being frightened that her husband would leave her that the thought of leaving him never entered her mind. Before we started her regression, she made it very clear what she wanted out of it—she was determined to find proof in a past life that she really belonged with this man and that she was justified in her belief that someday he would change and they'd be happy together. What we uncovered was far more significant. In one previous life in what was then Persia, her mother had died in childbirth and her father, having no interest in a girl-child, had left her on the bank of a river to drown. In a subsequent life, as a Spanish soldier in the Spanish-American War, her company, overpowered in a surprise Cuban attack, fled, leaving her to be captured and tortured for eleven horrible days before she was executed. While she was still under hypnosis, I asked her if anything from those lives sounded familiar in her present life. She answered immediately: the terror of being abandoned, and a belief that abandonment ultimately means death. Thanks to her own discoveries through her own past-life experiences, she gradually recognized that her current choices were only rubbing salt in old wounds rather than healing them. Less than six months later she called back asking for help of a much more productive kind, and my ministers and I were happy to find her a therapist and a shelter in which she safely and successfully recovered from her vicious sixteen-year marriage. One step at a time she built a fulfilling life of independence, freedom, and self-esteem and is now a tireless volunteer at a domestic-abuse crisis hotline.

It never ceases to amaze me that after all these years and all these regressions, there are still as many surprises in store for me as there are for my clients. If you saw my pay-per-view broadcast in June of this year, you saw me experience a career first. I was doing a past-life regression on a heavyset blond woman named Colleen, who recalled a previous incarnation in Africa that was ended by a lion attack in which the lion, like most big cats, started its kill with a fatal bite to her throat. She then began describing where she was and what she saw following that "death." At first, as she talked about green hills and a building of some kind with a thatched roof, I assumed she was telling me about The Other Side, which so many clients do during their regressions. But before I knew it she said she was in Ireland, watching the residents of that building. Women in white aprons. Children. Lots of children. No men around, anywhere. And, to Colleen's obvious sadness, while she could see these women and children so clearly, they couldn't see her. They never noticed her at all, as if she wasn't even there. She wanted very much to join them and be a part of the group, but she knew that "for some reason" she couldn't do that, nor could she leave—she was stuck there, an outsider, seemingly invisible, desperately unhappy and unable to leave for what she kept saying was "a long time, such a long time." It was all very confusing to her until I finally asked, "Would it mean anything to you if I said the word *earthbound?*" She simply replied, "Yes."

In other words, Colleen was recalling a long-ago, lost, hollow nightmare of being a ghost, trapped between dimensions at an Irish-Catholic orphanage. I've talked to many present-day ghosts, but I had never met a former ghost during a regression, and I'm sure I was more mesmerized by it than Colleen was. After all, she had no way of knowing that she was providing me with a singular experience. She was really quick, though, to make a connection between that awful sensation of being silently, invisibly earthbound in the past and her current, admittedly urgent, need for attention, to the point of even deliberately taking up a lot of physical space to make herself as hard to ignore as possible.

It turned out to be almost an afterthought that for most of her life, before her regression, Colleen suffered from sudden, terrifying throat spasms that made it impossible for her to breathe or swallow. Doctors have been unable to find the cause, let alone the cure. But for years Colleen has kept a friend on twenty-four-hour-a-day notice, so that if a spasm hits, she can dial this friend and simply pound the phone receiver on a table, alerting the friend that it's Colleen, in need of paramedics but unable to call them herself. As of this writing, not once since we uncovered the past-life memory of her throat being literally ripped out has Colleen ever had another one of those potentially dangerous spasms.

Another gratifying two-cures-for-the-price-of-one regression occurred with Stewart, an Englishman in his late forties, who told me at the beginning of our session that he was plagued by a couple of chronic problems. One was a recurring sharp pain in his chest despite years of tests showing that he's enviably healthy, without a single physiological problem in his chest or anywhere else. The other was an unusually oppressive fear of death that didn't become noticeable until his forty-first birthday, which he dismissed as a typical midlife-crisis symptom but couldn't seem to shake. By the end of our session he'd experienced two past lives, one in the pre-Civil War South that ended with a gunshot to the heart by a political rival when he was forty-two, and one in Austria when he died at the age of forty-three from what we would recognize today as lung cancer. He still drops me a note every few months to say his chest pains are nonexistent, and while he can't say he's looking forward to death, it's not even on his top ten list of fears anymore, let alone something that preoccupies him as it did when his cell memory reacted to being in a body in its early forties.

In each of these cases, then, from Leigh to Colleen to Stewart, and thousands of others like them, the spirit mind, finding itself in a physical body again, was sending signals to every cell based on that spirit's past experiences. "When I'm in a physical body, I'm abandoned by someone I trust." "When I'm in a physical body, I suffer a catastrophic throat trauma, after which I'm regarded as nonexistent." "When I'm in a physical body, I die in my early forties from fatal problems in the chest area." If you find yourself developing a sudden phobia over something that never especially bothered you before, or if some chronic physical problem develops that doctors seem to have a hard time diagnosing, you might consider the distinct possibility that it's cell memory in action, reacting to a past life that only interferes with this life to the extent that you allow it.

By the way, I do need to add one very important reminder: Please don't ever let any psychic, including me, become a substitute for a qualified member of the medical community. I work *with* literally hundreds of doctors and psychiatrists throughout the country, not *instead* of them, and as powerful as the effect of cell memory can be, it isn't the answer to every physical or emotional problem you might be having.

Birthmarks

You would think that with decades of evidence about past lives in general and cell memory in particular, I might have come up with a passing curiosity all by myself on the subject of birthmarks. You'd be wrong. I hadn't given them a single thought until a few years ago, when a neurologist friend asked for my input on his efforts to explore a possible connection between birthmarks and congenital illnesses. He was having no luck, but because of my extensive interest in my clients' health issues, he wondered if I would see what I could come up with, if anything, before he abandoned the theory altogether.

I didn't have any more luck than he did finding a link between birthmarks and congenital illness. Thanks to his broaching the subject, though, I found a completely different significance to birthmarks that continues to be an intriguing facet of my work with past-life regressions to this day.

It started with a client named Billy, who wasn't suffering from any illnesses at all, congenital or otherwise. He was interested in exploring his past lives in search of anyone he might be connected to in this life. While that particular pursuit was unsuccessful, we had a fascinating session, focused primarily on his incarnation as an American Indian that ended when he bled to death from a knife wound a couple of inches from his right knee. When the session was over and he was getting ready to leave, I suddenly remembered my neurologist friend and, purely as an afterthought, said, "By the way, do you happen to have any birthmarks?" He nodded, casually pulled up his pant leg, and showed me an angry-looking puncture-wound-shaped discoloration a couple of inches beneath his right knee.

On very rare occasions I run across a client I call a "somnambulist," which in the general world is a synonym for a sleepwalker but during regressions I use as a way to describe someone who goes so deeply "under" that they have no awareness of what they're saying and no memory of what they said when they're awake again. I wasn't aware that Billy was a somnambulist until that moment, when he became awkward and more than a little confused about how openly I was gaping at his leg. He truly had no idea why I was so fascinated by his birthmark until I played back his description of the wound that had killed him in another lifetime and he realized how much the birthmark looked like a scar of that wound.

One "coincidental" birthmark was hardly enough to send me cartwheeling around the room. At most, it piqued my curiosity, and I began casually asking clients at the end of regressive hypnosis sessions if they happened to have a birthmark. Of those who did, not just sixty percent, or seventy-five percent, or eighty percent had birthmarks that corresponded exactly to a critical or fatal wound they'd revealed on tape from a past life—a full ninety-eight percent of them did. Even that wouldn't necessarily have impressed me if I'd asked about birthmarks at the beginning of those sessions, which might somehow have planted a suggestion in them to make up a connection to please themselves or me during the regression. But after the fact, when their stories had been recorded and they weren't expecting the birthmark question at all, I would have been a fool to ignore such an overwhelming percentage of precisely placed birthmarks or to write them off as "coincidences."

A man with a clover-shaped red-brown birthmark in the middle of his chest, who had been executed for treason by a French firing squad; a man with a perfect dark circle behind his left ear, whose jealous wife had shot him in the head while he slept; a woman with a slender six-inch-long white mark across the side of her neck, who had been hanged as a suspected witch during the insane Salem trials; a man with a subtle row of three small red birthmarks like a short dotted line above his elbow, whose arm had been amputated at exactly that place as a child in a previous life in Indonesia; my files are full of documented stories like these, and I'm sure that the same wound-birthmark connections among my regression clients will continue as long as I continue to ask that last simple question, "By the way, do you have a birthmark?"

I'm sure my findings haven't been all that helpful to my neurologist friend who inspired this exploration in the first place, but I'm eternally grateful to him for the added dimension he, and birthmarks, have contributed to my passionate research into cell memory.

The Exercise

In my book *The Other Side and Back,* in a chapter entitled "Life after Life: How to Discover Your Own Past Lives," I included a lengthy and very effective exercise for performing your own regressions, preferably with the help of a friend. Rather than repeat it here, I'll give you a meditation that you can accomplish in less time and by yourself, that will at least give you a glimpse into the rich, amazing history of your spirit's journey and help you uncover and let go of any pain and fear you're carrying from a past life that might be holding you back in this one.

To prepare for this beautiful visit to your own legacy, I want you to surround yourself with the white light of the Holy Spirit and then, in a magnificent aura around that white light, a glow of deep purple, the royal color of God who created you, God whose genetic flame burns inside you, God who will guide you safely back down the path you've already traveled, to assure you that you have lived an eternity, you will live an eternity, and in our lives there is truly no end. You close your eyes and feel a legion of protection assemble around you—your Spirit Guide, a host of white-winged Angels, silently gathering to promise that with every step you take until your return, no danger, only joy, will come to you. You don't need to see this sacred army. You feel their presence, their divine unconditional love wrapping itself around your body, a warm safe cloak, impenetrable but weightless as glistening gossamer. You slowly stand, energized and confident, and feel the hem of your cloak whisper gently against your ankle. "You will never be alone," it reminds you. "Your Spirit Guide and Angels are with you, loving you, blessing this journey, blessing you for having the courage to witness your immortality."

You begin to walk, pulling your cloak more securely around you as, ahead of you, a silver tube appears, its opening large enough for you to step inside. It welcomes you, thrills you, fills you with the excitement of knowing that at its end wait secrets that are just for you and will change your view of yourself and your spirit forever. Your strides are strong and sure as you move to the inviting entrance of the silver tube, and without fear you cross its threshold. The instant your foot touches the cool, firm floor inside, this gorgeous silver tube begins to vibrate, shaking loose from its curved walls and ceiling a shower of glitter, a dusting of tiny silver-green sparkles so soft and fine that they're absorbed into your skin as they cover you. Your body and your spirit, hungry for nourishment and healing, joyfully consume this twinkling haze of purity, and you notice that with every new step you take you feel stronger, more powerful, more connected to your vital God-center than ever before. Energized, exhilarated with curiosity about what lies ahead, you begin to run. Your cloak of protection from your Spirit Guide and Angels, now sparkling with that same silver-green glitter, billows merrily around you as you run, closer and closer to the thrilling surprises that wait at the end of this miraculous glistening silver tube.

The tube widens, signaling that you're almost to the exit, when you look ahead and realize that everything that lies ahead is shrouded in a heavy white mist, hanging in the warm air, blocking your view. Your step slows, and for just an instant you're hesitant and a little afraid, tempted to turn back. But your fingers lightly touch the cloak that embraces you, and you hear from those loving voices again. "We are with you . . . blessing you for having the courage to witness your immortality." A sacred promise, too full of love to doubt. You take a breath and inch forward into the heavy cloud of mist and find yourself almost laughing with relief. It's safe and harmless, nothing but an opaque veil that momentarily blocks your vision but not your movement, and as your steps become confident again you know that this veil is all that's ever stood between you and a glimpse of your spirit's rich history. This veil, this quiet mist, was never there to stop you; only your fear and your lack of faith have done that. But now, protected, unafraid, and surging with the same faith in God that He has always had in you, you move on through this low cloud toward your past.

Your reward for not turning back comes quickly as, beyond the mist, beyond the tube's wide exit, you begin to make out the impossibly exquisite sight of a beautiful golden bridge, glimmering in the dancing rays of a brilliant sun and spanning a clear blue rushing stream. You can't wait to get there. You feel lighter than air, your bare feet scarcely touching the smooth brick that leads you out of the tube and onto this strong arch, and you stop for a moment in the middle of the glistening bridge to look down and watch the crystal water dancing over the rocks along the stream's shoreline. The sound of this rush of pure blue is almost hypnotic, the audible glory of life and undisturbed nature, as perfect, searching, and eternally potent as your spirit.

Your hands reluctantly let go of the warm railing, and you force your gaze away from the stream to the land beyond the bridge that you haven't let yourself face until now. It takes your eyes a moment to adjust to the light of the bright sun on the view ahead. When you're finally able to focus, you catch your breath, almost afraid to believe that the mystical vision past the stream and the golden bridge is real, but knowing it is. You blink back the tears that momentarily blur this place that your con-

scious mind is sure it's never seen before but your spirit mind recognizes as home.

Mountains. Desert. A hut in a quiet clearing in a vast forest. A quaint neighborhood from a time gone by, its cobblestone streets lined with gaslit lamps. A village filled with bustling, colorful open-air markets and ox-driven carts, the air thick with the sound of children playing nearby. A circle of covered wagons in the wilderness, gathered around a huge black pot over a fire, a simmering meal of fragrant stew. A harbor filled with tall ships and the smell of the sea. A cluster of crude igloos, huddled together in an endless field of ice and snow . . . Only you know the sight that greets you at this moment, and you know it's as much a part of you as your soul itself. You ask yourself for the name of this place where you are, and your answer comes immediately, in the very first word that comes into your mind.

As you begin walking off the bridge toward this strange, familiar place, you become aware of people noticing you, their faces filling with happy surprise as they recognize you. They hurry to greet you, and at first you can't identify them, dressed as they are in odd clothes from this other time and place you've found. But the closer they get, and the more you look past their clothing and faces that refuse to come into full focus, the more you recognize that these are spirits you deeply loved during your life in this place, and you step into the embrace of this magical reunion. You feel the tender touch of your mother from that time, the strong arms of your father, the comforting hugs of brothers, sisters, friends, your closest confidante back then, the uniquely charged intimacy of your lover's hand as it takes yours. The overwhelming truth washes over you in strong, sacred waves: You knew these people, you know them now, your spirit has yearned to see them again, and your love for each other, a persistent whisper in your soul's reality, is as powerful and eternal as life itself.

Elated to be with you but knowing it's too soon for you to stay, they guide you gently back toward the bridge, to the edge of the crystal stream. You understand their purpose, and trusting them, you lean forward slightly and look down into the water to find your reflection staring back at you. Not the "you" that entered the silver tube and took those first steps onto the golden bridge, but the you that lived in this place, in this time, among these loved and loving people. You study the reflection until you know it by heart and can bring it back through the tube with you, at first glance the reflection of a stranger but a body that was once home to the spirit that is yours and yours alone, and you appreciate it with all its beauty and its flaws as an essential part of who you are now.

You turn to face your loved ones again, their kisses light and tender against your cheeks as, without sadness, you say goodbye, confident in your certainty that now that you've found your way, you can come back whenever you like to visit this or any other place in the cherished memories of your spirit. Their love, the comfort of their embrace, the deep, dear familiarity of this time and this home, and the reflection that looked back at you from the sparkling stream will stay with you long after you've left to return to the time you call "today," and as you walk back across the golden bridge and into the glittering silver tube again, you know beyond all doubt that in these few short minutes your spirit has been nourished, healed, and allowed to soar to its sacred birthright of eternity.

THE AFFIRMATION

"Today I embrace all the love, wisdom, and comfort from all my past lives on this earth, and I release all negativity, fear, illness, and uncertainty from those same lives into the white light of the Holy Spirit, so that in liberating myself from any harmful cell memory I can remove these unnecessary barriers that stand between me and the center of my eternal spirit, which is the God who created it."

4

Contacting The Other Side

The spirits of our loved ones from The Other Side are with us all the time, watching over us, trying to communicate, hoping to somehow get our attention to prove to us that they're very much alive and that our fear of death is groundless. All we have to do to recognize those spirits is develop our tools, our open-minded awareness, and our faith in the God-center that burns inside us and keeps us eternally connected to each other and to our Father.

The paradise of Home, where our departed loved ones reside, is right here among us, just three short feet above our ground level. The only reason we don't readily perceive its presence is that it exists at a much higher frequency than we do. I've often used the analogy of the blades on an electric fan. When the fan is running at its lowest speed, we can see the blades clearly, but at its highest speed the blades seem to disappear. To believe spirits don't exist because we can't see them amounts to believing an electric fan running at its highest speed no longer has blades. But frequency levels aside, there is no difference between us here on earth and the spirits on The Other Side. In fact, "they" are "us," and "we" are "them," temporarily separated by simple physics but, I promise you, paying regular visits to each other, limited by nothing but our own reluctance to accept any news that seems too good to be true.

To understand the spirit world, it's important to understand that The Other Side isn't just where we'll go when this lifetime ends. It's also where each of us came from, our real Home between our occasional trips to this rough school called earth. Our spirits are on an eternal journey between here and The Other Side, constantly learning and growing toward the highest joy our Creator intended. What we on earth think of as birth and death are nothing but the mechanics by which we enter and leave the body we've chosen to occupy while we're here. We no more cease to exist when we vacate our bodies than we cease to exist when we vacate a house we've lived in and move on to another one. The only difference is, when we vacate our bodies, what we move on to is another dimension, as utterly familiar to our spirit minds as this world is now. And while we may not be consciously aware of it, our spirits, having had an eternity of practice, know exactly how to travel back and forth between the two dimensions, no matter which one we happen to be living on at the time. So of course we spirits communicate with each other. It's just a matter of paying attention.

Verbal Messages from The Other Side

I've seen and heard spirits from The Other Side all my life, and thank God I had my brilliantly psychic Grandmother Ada there to teach me the basics of what to watch and listen for. Skeptic and passionate researcher that I am, I've spent my adulthood refining and expanding on those basics and discovering the fascinating variety of ways in which those from Home are constantly saying to their loved ones on earth, "You don't have to miss me, I'm right here!"

Verbal contact from The Other Side comes in two ways: actual voices, which usually get distorted into a high and frankly annoying chirping sound as they cross dimensions, and infused knowledge, which is simply information passed directly from one mind to another, those things you suddenly "just know" without having a clue how or why you know it.

An example of voice contact from Home that still makes me chuckle occurred on one of my recent television appearances. A distraught man in the audience stood up and asked if I could please tell him if his recently deceased mother had any messages for him. I could see her standing behind his left shoulder and described her in detail, right down to her habit of unconsciously running her fingers through her hair. He confirmed the description almost impatiently, as if any idiot would know what she looked like, and repeated his request for a message. Her high-pitched voice began chirping incessantly in my ear, and at her insistence I asked him, "Who is Stephan?" He stared blankly at me and shrugged, but she kept right on chirping, so I repeated, "She wants me to tell Stephan she's watching over him. Who is Stephan?" His blank stare continued. If you've seen me in action, you know that when I'm given information from The Other Side, I won't back down, right or wrong, until it's at least been acknowledged. Besides, she was starting to give me a headache. So, even though I wasn't getting so much as a glimmer of recognition from this man, I asked one more time, admittedly exasperated, "Sir, please, will you just tell me who Stephan is?" He paused. It finally hit him. "Oh," he said. *"I'm* Stephan." You think this job is easy?

You certainly don't have to be a professional psychic to hear spirit voices. In fact, countless clients have heard them and simply not understood what they were or where they were coming from. It's imperative to add that these are *not* the voices that purportedly tell psychotics and criminals to do terrible things. Don't forget, The Other Side is a paradise of absolute love, so spirit voices who are truly from Home are incapable of aiding and abetting any cruel thoughts and actions, and those spirit voices are nothing to be afraid of. But I've had plenty of "civilian" witnesses to spirits' apparent special enjoyment of imprinting their voices on audiotape. One client's Spirit Guide clearly uttered the client's name on audiotape during a regression. A notoriously protective dog I owned in a past life has been heard barking furiously on tape at several of my haunting investigations, even though none of us at the actual site heard a single sound at the time. Several clients' tape recorders simultaneously captured the sound of heartbreaking wailing and crying in a completely silent room one night when my Spirit Guide, Francine, was giving a lecture about the crucifixion of Christ. Never underestimate how opportunistic spirits are, ready to leap at any chance to let us know they're around, so it's not surprising that they'll happily take advantage of the magnetic property of audiotape when they want to be heard. Because of that, I recommend a simple exercise if you're curious about trying to hear their voices yourself:

Set up an audiocassette recorder in a room in your home other than where you sleep, so that you won't lie awake all night listening for some foreign noise. Before you fall asleep, surround yourself with the white light of the Holy Spirit for protection, then invite your Spirit Guide, your deceased loved ones, and any other spirits sent by God from The Other Side to visit during the night and leave their imprint on tape.

You may not get anything for several nights, weeks, or even months, and I can't encourage you enough to play back the tape only in the background of your normal activities. For one thing, it can be really boring. For another thing, if you listen too hard you could easily find yourself hearing noises and voices that simply aren't there. At best, you'll have success sooner or later and end up with a genuine recording of a visit from paradise. At worst, by simply providing spirits with this opportunity, you'll be acknowledging your blessed connection to The Other Side and the eternity of your own soul.

Infused knowledge from The Other Side is obviously faster and more subtle than voice communication. I use infused knowledge for everything from messages about misplaced objects, hidden wills, or journals and insurance policies, to the location of missing bodies of murder victims, the details of their deaths, and even the names of their killers. Rather than receiving a rush of words, I'm given this information in a flood of images instead, as quickly as I can describe them, knowing without knowing how I know, just certain that I'm not the source, only the tube through which that information is flowing.

I guarantee you've received infused knowledge yourself, from your Spirit Guide or a departed loved one, and mislabeled it as "instinct" or "a sudden impulse" or some awareness that "just came over you." It can be as trivial as answering the phone before it rings or as critical as an urgent compulsion to check on someone you love and discovering they're in serious trouble. Maybe most common of all is infused knowledge during sleep, when the cluttered conscious mind is out of the way and the spirit mind in the subconscious can communicate freely with other spirits. If you've ever gone to sleep with a problem on your mind and awakened with a solution without a clue where it came from, you've experienced infused knowledge from the loving, watchful spirits on The Other Side—it's that simple and that divine. Just for fun, try this:

For one short month, keep a journal of every "instinct" that comes to you, whether you follow it or not, and the outcome of your response to it. Add to it every question you were concerned about when you went to sleep that you have an answer to when you wake up. Don't review the journal until the end of that month. Then read it from start to finish. If you were paying attention, there will be more of these "instincts" and "brainstorms during the night" than you expected there to be, not to mention easier responses on your part and clearer outcomes than when your conscious mind agonizes over your problems. Dismiss the instincts and brainstorms as ordinary, or even take credit for them if it makes you more comfortable, but at least leave your mind just a tiny bit open to the fascinating possibility that, with surprising regularity, you're being given infused knowledge from The Other Side.

Physical Signs from The Other Side

Spirits can briefly manifest themselves in physical form among us as well, and again, the ability to see them is hardly limited to those of us whose lives are devoted to the psychic and spiritual world. Children and animals, who are the most psychic beings on earth, routinely see and react to spirits, gloriously unaware that traditional society thinks there's something inappropriate or suspect about that behavior. Adults commonly see spirits, too, they're just more reluctant to talk about it in public because, take it from me, being called "crazy" can start to get on your nerves after a while. I sat with a client a while ago whose husband appeared at the foot of her bed just hours after his violent death in a car fire, healthy, happy, and perfect, his smile reassuring her with exquisite love before he vanished again. She'd shared this blessed experience with her best friend, who dismissed it as a reaction to the sedative my client's doctor had prescribed. That must have been one strong sedative, causing such a realistic hallucination when my client hadn't even taken it yet.

I often wish those people whose motto seems to be "Any explanation *but* the spirit world" could talk to the countless "normal" members of my audiences who ask why I didn't introduce the tall woman with the dark braid who stood behind me onstage.

They're invariably shocked to hear that they've just described my Spirit Guide, Francine, especially since many of them have never heard of her. Other members of those same audiences, who may know exactly who Francine is, will swear I was on that stage by myself, proving that she wasn't some cleverly rigged special effect.

Spirits who appear with my clients during readings frequently communicate through pantomime. They'll help me confirm their identity by indicating the part of their body most directly involved in their cause of death, they'll demonstrate some subtle affectation that will help my client recognize them, and most frequently they'll act out something that means nothing to me but everything to the loved one they've dropped by my office to visit. One of my favorites was a vibrant, dark-haired young man who appeared very clearly with my client, his sister, who was struggling with her grief over losing him in a motorcycle accident. He kept enthusiastically tugging on his left earlobe, much like the "sounds-like" signal in a game of charades. I had no clue what the significance was, so I simply duplicated the gesture and said, "Your brother's doing this.

What does this mean?" My client was visibly shaken, and then thrilled. Her brother, she explained, wore an earring in his left ear that he treasured but their parents hated. They refused to let him be buried wearing it but gave it to my client as a keepsake instead. The day before our reading, she'd had her left ear pierced, and she proudly pulled back her hair to show me the tiny sparkling diamond stud that would be her way of always keeping him with her. He was clearly showing her, through me, that he knew she was wearing it and that it made him very happy.

The most common way for the spirit world to get our attention, though, is to manipulate objects around us just enough that if we're paying attention and know what to look for, we'll have the comforting assurance that our loved ones are visiting. They'll turn lights off and on, send televisions on spontaneous cycles through all their channels, stop clocks, make phones and doorbells ring, play music boxes, activate kitchen and laundry appliances, lay photographs of themselves facedown or turn them backward, scatter handfuls of coins in unlikely places, move our car keys from wherever we *know* we put them, take an unmistakable seat on the sofa or the edge of the bed to the point of leaving a slight indentation—again, they love attention, they're very inventive, and they'll do almost anything to say, "Hey, wake up and smell the coffee, I'm right here!"

By the way, it's no coincidence that so much spirit activity involves electrical objects and occurs during rainstorms or in the early morning hours before dawn. Electricity and water, in the form of rain or humidity or dew, are conductors of energy, after all, and spirits are energy. Conductors aren't essential to spirits' ability to visit us, but they can definitely make the trip between dimensions easier. There's also no coincidence in the fact that candles are such a traditional part of spiritual and religious rituals. It turns out that spirits are unable to see artificial lighting, but they'll instantly spot and be attracted by candlelight.

In that same journal in which you jot down your "instincts" and "brainstorms," I want you to make a quick note of anything unusual that happens around your house, no matter how trivial it seems at the time—a light or appliance turned on that you're sure you turned off, your keys in some other place than where you thought you left them, a photograph or vase of flowers or any random object moved slightly from where you remembered it to be, anything that makes you pause for a moment and think no more and no less about it than "That's odd." Don't watch so closely that you become preoccupied with it, just get in the habit of paying attention while you go about your day and then writing down anything even slightly out of the ordinary. Then, every month or two, read what you've written. I have a feeling you'll be pleasantly surprised at how many "out of the ordinary" things are going on right under your nose, and therefore how many spirits from Home are around you trying to say hello.

Spirit Contact among the Living

His name was Bradley. He was in his mid-twenties, bright, well dressed, and soft spoken, and I liked him from the moment he entered my office. I knew before he said a word that he was very upset, and he looked shocked when I greeted him with "Tell me why you're so worried about your mother."

It seems that a few nights earlier, Bradley

had been awakened out of a sound sleep by his mother's voice, repeating his name over and over again in a loud whisper. He sat bolt upright, her voice so real that he fully expected to see her standing beside his bed, despite the fact that she lived two thousand miles away. It almost shocked him more that she wasn't there than if she had been, and he was so convinced of what he'd heard that he got out of bed and looked around until he was convinced that he was alone in his apartment as usual. He thought about calling her to make sure she was all right, but even with the difference in time zones, it was still awfully early in the morning where she was. So he finally did what most people would have done—he talked himself into thinking it must have been one of those incredibly vivid dreams and went back to bed. He was too busy at work all morning to give the incident any more thought, until his mother called his office, which she rarely did, and said, "I feel a little silly asking, but by any chance did I wake you up this morning?"

Very startled, he managed a simple "Yes, you did."

"I was afraid of that. I'm sorry," she replied. "I was meditating about you, and somehow or other I suddenly just knew you'd heard me."

Bradley's mother was a normal, healthy, down-to-earth, smalltown conservative midwestern woman in her seventies, who was very active in her local Presbyterian church. "Meditating" for her was a half hour in her favorite chair to start her day, enjoying the silence, collecting her thoughts, studying her beloved Bible, and saying her morning prayers. Bradley had never heard of her spirit, or anyone's, leaving its body and traveling around the country dropping in on loved ones, and not knowing what to make of it, he was afraid that an event that dramatic might have been a predeath omen of some kind.

As I assured him, the truth is that astral travel, which is *exactly* the spirit taking temporary trips away from the body it inhabits, is common, among the trained and the untrained—look at Bradley's mother, who'd accomplished it very powerfully without having a clue what it was. If you've ever had an unusually vivid, sequential dream, either a daydream or a dream while you slept, or thought you were wide awake and moving around when your medical charts swore you were extremely ill, unconscious, or in a coma, I'm willing to bet your spirit was astrally romping around all over the place having a great time, with your body and your conscious mind conveniently out of its way.

One of the dearest clients I ever met was a woman in her sixties named Bess. During her reading she mentioned in passing that she'd been finding little piles of coins in the oddest places throughout her house. She'd eliminated every logical explanation she could come up with about where the coins were coming from and wondered if I had any theories.

The instant she asked the question, the spirit responsible for those coins made a brief appearance beside her. His name was Dan, he was tall, in his early seventies, thin, with a full head of wild white hair, and his eyes were a remarkable pale brown. She looked more and more confused as I described him. She knew exactly who he was—even though they had both married other people, Bess and Dan were the great loves of each other's lives. What confused her was that Dan was suffering from advanced Parkinson's disease but was still very much alive.

This story illustrates beautifully that even when the body it resides in is ill or disabled, the power of the spirit is never diminished. Often, in fact, the more advanced the disease, the more frequent the spirit's astral trips to visit people and places it misses—even if the disease is a mental one, which only affects the conscious mind but can't touch the spirit mind in the subconscious. If you have a loved one who's suffering from anything from Alzheimer's disease to a severe stroke to a coma to an advanced neurological affliction, never doubt that their wide awake, eternal spirits hear and thrive in all the joyful affirmations you can offer. And don't forget to watch for signs that their spirit is visiting you, loving you, and reassuring you of your shared immortality, even when their body and their conscious mind are no longer able.

Visiting The Other Side

We don't have to wait for loved ones from Home to visit us when we get lonely for them. We can go to The Other Side for visits, too, through astral travel during meditation or sleep, and, I promise, make real contact. There's no need to worry about getting trapped over there before our time, or not being able to return to our body. The truth is, our spirits visit Home on an average of three or four times a week while we're asleep, we just don't consciously remember. The only difference between those unplanned trips and the deliberate ones we're all capable of is a little advance notice to God and our Spirit Guide that we're coming, so they can notify whoever it is we're hoping to see.

The main reason for prearranging a meeting with a loved one who's passed on, instead of dropping in and surprising them, is that no matter what their age when they left this earth, everyone on The Other Side is thirty years old. Whether it's a two-year-old child we lost or a ninety-year-old grandparent, they're thirty in their natural spirit life at Home, and we could easily have trouble recognizing them. When they come here, or when they're expecting us there, they return to the form that's familiar to us so that we don't greet them with a blank, disappointed "Who are you?"

So before you begin your visit to The Other Side, settle into a relaxed position in a quiet place, surround yourself with the white light of the Holy Spirit, and ask God and your Spirit Guide to alert the loved one you miss that you're on your way, and you'll be watching for them through what we call "The Window to The Other Side."

The Exercise

Close your eyes and take a deep breath, and sense that there is a divine golden light swirling gently through the Holy Spirit's white light that always surrounds you. Around this magnificent blend of gold and white, a glistening silver egg appears, almost iridescent opal, a prismed rainbow, cocooning you and your protective, sacred lights into one perfect self-contained embryo. As you bask in the glorious oval that will take you safely on your journey, the silver prism around you expands the gold and white lights into a gleaming mosaic of green, blue, rose, and shades of purple, and you feel every cell of your body being bathed in healing, spirituality, and the infinite love of the Father and Mother God.

You lift your face up to receive every beam of these magnificent lights. Your skin warms at their slightest nurturing touch, and hungry for more, you stand and lift your arms to welcome their embrace into the core of your soul. You are cleansed, whole, and strong, and you're suddenly aware, in a rush of joy, that you're not alone, as the visions of the Father and Mother God Themselves take brilliant holy shape on either side of you, your constant and most divine Companions and Guides, blessing you, loving you.

In the awesome company of your Creators, you look ahead of yourself again, to see the iridescent silver egg dissolve and a crystal-clear window appear, its huge pane gracefully arched, pastel lights dancing around its delicate beveled border. And through this window, your eyes fall with awed gratitude on a lush green meadow, surrounded by distant flower-covered hills, and you gasp at the familiar, cherished sight of The Other Side. Of Home.

Slowly, across the meadow, out of the soft rose-colored mist, all the loved ones of this lifetime who have passed appear and begin walking quietly toward the window where you stand, smiling, peaceful, full of transcendent rapture, arm in arm, united in their love for you and for God. You see their footprints in the dew-covered green. You smell freshly cut grass. You savor every sensation of this exquisite reunion, knowing the memory of it has already etched itself into your soul so profoundly that remnants of it will linger long after you awake again. Your loved ones come closer . . . closer . . . overjoyed to see you but not surprised, because you gave them time to prepare before your journey began.

They stop, just a few feet from the window, and you can feel through the glass the sheer force of their loving gratitude for your arrival. You and they know it's not time for you to stay, not yet, and as you meet their eyes the absolute certainty rushes through you that when that time does come, you will go with serene exultation, and that they'll all be waiting to embrace you and welcome you Home.

The loved one you most hoped to see steps forward from the crowd and reaches out their hand to you. You reach out as well, and to your amazement your hand passes safely and unharmed through the cool glass, leaving the rest of the window around it fully intact. Your hands touch, lightly at first, then firm and strong as they clasp together, electric, a power surge as two dimensions unite in love. You look into their eyes at long last, the sight you've been yearning for, your favorite sight in all the world, and at that moment every word, every unfinished thought and act, spills out of you into their dear, safe soul. "I love you." "I miss you." "I'm sorry." "I didn't get to say goodbye." "I forgive you." There's nothing you can't say, nothing you hold back, and with every truth you speak you feel your heart grow lighter.

Their eyes soften with compassion. Their smile widens, and their hand strengthens its hold on yours. Without making a sound, they absorb your heart's burdens into the bliss of Home. "I understand," they silently promise, "and I love you." You have never been so sure of anything as you are that they've just given you the same truth you gave to them, and that the peace they've found on The Other Side, the peace that transcends words and earthly hurts and missteps, the peace that ultimately comes Home to soar among the Angels, has just healed your soul.

All said, all resolved, you squeeze the hand of your loved one in farewell, secure that you'll visit again, that they'll visit you, and that you'll be together again when you've finished your spirit's work on earth. There's no sadness between you as your hands part, and you can still feel their touch as your hand withdraws safely back through the crystal window again.

You smile as the iridescent silver egg slowly enfolds you again, and as it returns you to your starting place you thank God for this blessed reunion and for the peace of mind you know will stay with you from this moment on, to share with your loved ones here, whose hands will reach for yours through that window someday and find it waiting, more strong and sure than ever.

THE AFFIRMATION

"My spirit and the spirits of all I love have been blessed by our Creator with eternal life, and through my faith and His sacred design, there is no distance too great or silence too deep to ever keep us apart. I feel the very real presence of my loved ones' spirits, both here and at Home, every moment of every day, just as surely and powerfully as they feel my loving presence with them."

P.S.

The news cliché "This just in!" leaps to mind.

Remember my mentioning that when I'm writing, events seem to present themselves that are directly relevant to whatever subject I happen to be working on?

I finished this chapter and found myself lonely for my father, so I got out my favorite picture of him and was smiling at it when my grandson Willy, age two and a half, strolled in, looked at the photo, and said, "Who is that, Bagdah?" (He and his sister Angelia have never called me anything but Bagdah.)

I explained that it was my father, Willy's great-grandfather, and that I knew Daddy would have loved Willy very much if he hadn't had to go Home before Willy got here.

Willy playfully nudged me, looked up at me, grinned, and said, "That's my girl."

Ask anyone who ever saw me and Daddy together if there's one special signal of love they remember between us, and they'll tell you it was how he'd always nudge me, grin, and say, "That's my girl."

My two-and-a-half-year-old grandson, on the other hand, has never said the words *That's my girl* to anyone in his life, let alone his Bagdah, let alone while nudging me and grinning as no one but Daddy ever did.

To the list of ways in which The Other Side communicates with us, apparently I need to add that sometimes departed loved ones speak through the willing, innocent, guilelessly psychic mouths of children.

Thanks, Daddy. Message received.

5

Forgiveness

It was Alexander Pope who wrote, "To err is human, to forgive divine." I agree. To forgive is divine. The catch is, the only divine Being is God.

Which leaves the rest of us with a lot of tough issues to work through on the subject of forgiveness. As God's children, are we always morally obligated to "forgive those who trespass against us"? Do we have the right to expect forgiveness, no matter what we've done, if we ask for it nicely? If we're spiritually required to forgive with every apology, are we sending the message that no behavior is off limits, as long as we say we're sorry afterward? Is there such a thing as being too quick, or too slow, to forgive? How many times can we be expected to forgive the same person for the same act? And what if, no matter how hard we try and how spiritual we are, there are things we simply can't forgive? Does that make *us* unforgivable in God's eyes?

See what I mean? Forgiveness is much too complicated a process to be reduced to a black-and-white rule that "good people forgive and bad people don't." And make no mistake about it, it is a *process* that depends on the actions of both the person being asked to forgive and the person who's asking forgiveness. It is a choice, a gift *"for giving,"* with sincerity or not at all, and ironically it's the forgiver who receives the greater share of that gift.

On Forgiving

By definition and design, we're living in an imperfect world, and while we're here, it's a guarantee that wrongs will be done to us and we'll be faced with the dilemma over and over again of whether or not to forgive those wrongs. One of the hard parts of the dilemma is that it's so highly personal—only we can make up our own lists of what's forgivable and what's not. And even then, those lists are likely to be more flexible than we expected when we mentally wrote them. Something we're sure we could never forgive becomes a different story when we find ourselves actually confronted with that situation, while something else we would have sworn we'd get over easily becomes surprisingly insurmountable. Another hard part, which we don't always like to acknowledge, is that we're all going to want to be forgiven from time to time, and *we have no right to ask for anything in this life that we refuse to give.*

Anytime we face a serious question of forgiveness, we owe it to the person who's asking, and certainly to ourselves, to include some basic considerations in our ultimate decision.

- **Compassion** belongs at the heart of every action we take toward every other living being on this planet, and that definitely includes forgiveness. I wish the Golden Rule hadn't become such a cliché that we've stopped really listening to it, because it sums up the definition of compassion so perfectly: "Do unto others as you would have them do unto you." And hard as this is to believe sometimes, compassion is an inherent part of human nature. On The Other Side, where there's no negativity, no greed or jealousy or ego, and no need for laws to keep our behavior in line, compassion is as natural to us as breathing. Compassion when it comes to forgiveness simply means hearing out the other person, putting ourselves in their position, and taking all of their circumstances into account, including their strengths and weaknesses. They have them, you can count on it. So do you. So do we all.

- **Motive matters.** It just does. There are deliberate actions, and then there are accidents, acts of carelessness and ignorance, and rash moments of thoughtlessness. The most awesome historical example of taking motive into account is Christ's plea from the cross on behalf of his executioners, "Father, forgive them, for they know not what they do." (Luke 23:34) I have to admit, that passage, like all of Jesus' sacred life, has always seemed like the ultimate path to aspire to in every way, but I wasn't sure many of us could realistically expect it of ourselves. Then I met a client named Leland, whose young wife had been killed by a drunk driver on the way home from a wedding they'd all attended. Leland was grieving deeply, but he'd forgiven the drunk driver. I asked him how he managed that. "I matched him drink for drink at that wedding," he told me. "It could just as easily have been me who killed someone that night. And he didn't mean for this to happen any more than I would have." Believe me, this isn't my way of advocating sympathy for drunk drivers. I applaud zero tolerance on that issue. But if that client, in the face of his loss, can recognize that the only difference between him and that drunk driver was luck, not motive, I'm pretty sure the rest of us can try harder to do the same.

- **A sense of proportion** can rescue us from our own pettiness if we'll let it. You know people, and so do I, who treat an unreturned phone call from a friend, or someone taking "their" parking space, or bad taste in Christmas gifts, with exactly the same gravity as if their child had been kidnapped or their parents murdered. When we return Home at the end of our lifetime, one of our first experiences is to review every moment of that lifetime at the Scanning Machine. I think of the Scanning Machine every time I'm tempted to overreact, and wonder if I'll really enjoy watching myself refuse to forgive a loved one for forgetting my birthday or waiter for bringing me the wrong order, in the middle of a life full of real crises and serious betrayals that were much more deserving of my emotional energy.

- **The ultimate goal of forgiving is peace of mind—not theirs, *ours.*** We can kid ourselves all we want about how our decision to forgive someone is an act of generosity and proves what a fine human being we are. But the truth is, what we're after most, whichever way that decision goes, is a release from any negative power the event or the person in question has over us. Not only is it spiritually paralyzing to stay fiercely bound to someone or something that's hurt us, but it's also physically destructive. The scientific and medical worlds are starting to catch on that smoldering grudges and unresolved resentment take a measurable toll on our immune system and our cardiovascular system, just as any stress does. So whether it's forgiving or not forgiving that brings us peace and allows us to let go and move on, our health literally can't afford our getting stuck on emotional wounds without taking steps to help them heal.

- **Don't go through the motions of forgiveness for any other reason than complete sincerity.** Claiming to forgive and then continuing to punish or nag or hold the wrong over the person's head is, in its way, as destructive as whatever caused the problem to begin with. Heartfelt forgiveness is too serious and too valuable to be reduced to some manipulation tactic, some carrot to dangle, take away, and then dangle again to maintain a false sense of power over the person who wronged you. Don't forget, every time we remind someone of pain they put us through, we remind ourselves as well and either consciously or unconsciously relive the pain, which keeps us from moving on. Besides, sooner or later dangling that carrot is destined to stop working—figuratively speaking, no one likes carrots *that* much.

- **Love yourself and them enough to put conditions on your forgiveness.** In fact, I'm a big believer in not even discussing forgiveness until *after* the person has proved that whatever happened won't happen again, until they genuinely understand the impact of what they did and take steps to get to the bottom of why they did it so that they can insure a change for the better in their treatment of us. I don't want to hear "I'm sorry" about the same behavior more than once. It means I haven't learned from the experience and neither have they, and I promise, the charts we wrote before we came here were designed for us to learn, not to waste our time on earth refusing to move off of "square one."

One important postscript to our responsibility when it comes to forgiveness, by the way, that can make things much easier for us and those around us before it even becomes an issue: Each of us has our own priorities and our own sensitivities, and it's not fair to expect other people to guess what those are. The better we are at clarifying what's important to us and what we won't tolerate, the less likely we are to set ourselves up to be constantly irritated and faced with the decision of whether or not we're willing to forgive. If it hurts your feelings for your birthday to be forgotten, for example, let your family and friends know that and help them remember when it is. Don't just sit waiting to be angry and victimized if someone forgets, unless you can honestly say you've never forgotten the birthday of someone close to you. If you don't like people stopping by without calling first, don't assume everyone feels that way. They don't. Speak up before, not after, someone makes the mistake. If you can't stand tardiness, if you don't like getting phone calls before 8:00 A.M., if you don't appreciate being disturbed during your favorite TV show, if you have an aversion to Chinese food or jazz or discussing politics, make those "ground rules" clear. Demanding that everyone respect rules they know nothing about and then refusing to forgive them if they break one of those rules amounts to entrapment, and in that case the only person you should really be angry with is *you.*

On Asking for Forgiveness

We're going to make mistakes in this life, and from time to time, one way or another, we're going to hurt someone. The chart we wrote on The Other Side is designed to include those eventualities, not to give us permission but to give us challenges to overcome and learn from, partly by trying to make up for any pain we cause. Because all sides of forgiveness—giving it, receiving it, and refusing it—are basic and essential to the growth and ultimate grace of our spirit, no chart has ever been written that didn't demand attention to the lessons that only forgiveness makes possible. Inevitably, unless we're sociopaths, we'll be asking someone to forgive us. The question is, how can we increase our chances of being successful at it?

- **Take full responsibility, without adding insult to injury by offering a convenient**

list of excuses. Countless clients have sat in my office agonizing over having wronged someone they care about. I've learned through them, and through my own experience, that psychologists are absolutely right—saying, "I'm sorry," and then adding the word *but* cancels out the apology, unless what follows the "but" is something that couldn't be helped. "I'm sorry, but my car broke down" or "I'm sorry, but my flight was canceled" are worth listening to. Any variations on "I'm sorry, but you made me angry" and "I'm sorry, but I was upset" amount to "It's really your fault" or "I can behave any way I want when I'm unhappy." Remember, we chart mistakes to learn from them, and refusing to learn from them means we're charted to keep repeating them. How can we learn from them if we won't accept them as ours to begin with?

- **The harder it is to apologize, the sooner we should do it.** I've always found it confusing when people postpone offering an apology they know they owe with the excuse "I have my pride." Withholding an owed apology

makes us look both wrong and cowardly, and the longer we withhold that
apology, the longer we look wrong and
cowardly. Where's the pride in *that?*
And you and I know that it gets harder,
not easier, to apologize as time goes
on. That's one great reason to get it
over with. Another great reason is most
easily illustrated if we picture our life's
chart as a long-running television show,
various aspects of it airing in sequence
on different channels. Ideally, if our lives
are progressing as we charted them, we
can tune in to any channel at any time
and see action, movement, and events
unfolding, no matter how slowly or un-
evenly. But for every apology we owe
but haven't offered, there's a channel
on which there is no movement, and
instead the action is frozen at the exact
moment of that act for which we'd like
to be forgiven. The only way to reacti-
vate that channel, i.e., our chart, is to
bring that part of our lives up to date
with an apology so that we can move
forward again. Every minute we delay
is another minute the chart we planned
for ourselves is falling behind, which

amounts to nothing but wasted time and wasted emotional energy.

- **Forgiveness is a process, not a single act, and lasting forgiveness shouldn't come until that process is under way.** That way, when we promise, "It won't happen again," we can offer proof that there's reason to believe us. If, for example, we want to ask forgiveness for a loan we've made no effort to repay, we have no business asking empty handed. We need to ask while handing over at least some of the money and a schedule of when we'll pay the rest. Or, if the forgiveness involves bad behavior caused by substance abuse or seriously losing our temper, the apology needs to be accompanied by the news that we're already attending twelve-step meetings or a rehab clinic or anger-management classes. There's a huge difference between "I'm planning to" and "I already am." Not to mention the real chart-stopper "I'm going to try." "Trying" is one of the easiest ways in the world to avoid "doing." Until we're ready to do better than "try," we have no business expecting to be forgiven.

- **We have no legitimate right to resent the inevitable consequences of our actions.** Directly or indirectly, sooner or later, like it or not, there is always a consequence to everything we do, thanks to a powerful universal truth called "karma." *Karma* simply means "a balance of experience." We really do reap what we sow. Karma ultimately rewards goodness and punishes negativity. It's not a system of judgment inflicted on us by God. God doesn't judge or punish, He just loves. By choosing what our actions will or won't be, we create our own karma. So when the consequences set in, good or bad—and they will, we can count on it—the one person we have to thank or to blame is that person staring back at us from the mirror.

- **Remember, no one is obligated to accept our apology.** I'm not sure why that fact is so easy to forget, but for some reason we seem to assume that if we wrong someone and then say sincerely that we're sorry, they owe it to us to forgive us. No, they really don't. They're as free to make choices as we are, and that includes whether or not to care how sorry we might be and whether or not to give us the peace of mind that being forgiven makes possible.

The Unforgivable

Make no mistake about it, I am a devout humanitarian and Gnostic, which is the loving faith Christ practiced during his time on earth. (Obviously he couldn't have been a Christian, unless he discovered a way to follow himself.) I made an ironclad contract with God through my chart before I came here to leave this world better than I found it, and not a day goes by when I don't take steps toward fulfilling that contract. But be cruel and hurtful to someone I love, or to a child or animal or anyone who's unable to care for and defend themselves, and you'll see proof of my firm belief that some actions really are unforgivable.

As I said earlier, one of the biggest reasons to learn forgiveness is our own peace of mind and our own freedom from the emotional weight of harboring resentment. There are certain wrongs, crimes, and betrayals that would bring me no peace of mind to forgive, as long as I make sure to release any paralyzing bitterness over them and then use my residual anger toward the acts to accomplish something positive. There are no hard-and-fast rules about what's forgivable and what isn't. It's really a highly personal decision, and a choice only we can make, based on our own comfort level and our refusal to let our spiritual progress be stopped by an unforgivable act.

On a grand scale, there's no better example of putting the unforgivable to good use than John Walsh, who among other great accomplishments is the creator and host of television's *America's Most Wanted*. I make no secret of my enormous admiration for him, which I know a lot of you share. And most of you know his story. His beautiful little son Adam was kidnapped and murdered, and while he's sure he knows who committed this hideous crime, there was never an arrest, let alone a conviction. Has he forgiven the man who killed his child? Of course not. But rather than being consumed by bitterness over the unforgivable, he's let his rage propel him forward to create new legislation for children's rights, set up organizations to locate missing children, help countless victims find solace and justice, and be enormously responsible for the capture of almost seven hundred felons.

On a smaller, more anonymous scale, I recently worked with two brothers in their forties whose mother had recently passed away. It wasn't an ordinary case of family grief. In this case, their mother had badly abused them as children and then abandoned them to run off with her drug-addicted boyfriend. When they'd finally been reunited with her some twenty-five years later, she offered no apologies, only denial and excuses. In fact, if anything, she'd selfishly decided to make *herself* the victim in this heartbreaking story. What fascinated me was that both brothers, after going through identical childhood horrors, had become responsible, productive, generous, loving members of society and, even more amazingly, wonderful and attentive fathers. One had forgiven their mother completely. The other hadn't and never intended to. But both had made peace with their choices about forgiving her and were making the best possible use of those opposite decisions, which as far as I'm concerned means that they're both right and they've both earned the happiness that lies ahead for them.

And then there was Liza, who was in enormous turmoil when I met her. She had taken care of her elderly father until the end of his life ten months earlier, while her only sibling, her brother Max, hadn't visited or offered a dime of support during their father's long, painful, expensive illness. But Max did manage, with the help of a shady attorney and a few loopholes in the will, to cheat Liza out of the entire estate, with the exception of the one item she wanted most—their father's pocket watch, a gift from his grandfather and his most cherished possession. A few days after the funeral, Liza, resigned to Max's unfair legal victory, asked for the watch. Her brother smirked and replied, "You want the watch? Here's the watch." With which he threw it on the floor in front of her and stomped on it, shattering it into a million pieces. Ten months later, Liza was still in as much pain as she had been at that moment the watch was destroyed, the grief of losing her father almost easier than her agony over finding herself unable to forgive her brother for such a blatant act of meanness. "I'm a Christian," she kept saying, "and Max is the only family I have left. I keep telling myself it was just a watch, but I can't seem to get past this and make peace with him."

What I believe, and what I told Liza, is that on this imperfect earth, where we're all at different phases in our spirits' progress with our own lessons to learn, we're all likely to be confronted with an unforgivable act, committed by someone who's not as far along the path as we are. When and if that happens as it has to me—the answer isn't blaming ourselves, or offering insincere forgiveness that will make the other person feel better while we're consumed with resentment. The answer is whatever allows us to move on and do it productively. If that happens to be forgiveness, great. If it's too big for us to forgive, *put it into God's hands for His divine forgiveness, and then let it and that person go!*

Let's face it, we place other problems in God's hands when they're beyond our ability to solve them. Why should we hesitate to ask Him to lift a burden as heavy and as negative as forgiveness of the unforgivable, so that we can proceed with the positive, productive, healthy, spiritual, loving lives we all charted ourselves to lead?

Forgiveness from The Other Side

One of the most frequent sources of pain my clients bring to me is the issue of unfinished business between them and a deceased loved one, and their agonized fear that their loved one died without forgiving them for everything from an unsettled argument to an unpaid debt to an unkept promise.

A classic example is Lauren, who sat sobbing in my office a few months ago. Lauren and her mother, Eleanor, were great friends and very close, and when Eleanor began having some chronic, occasionally serious health problems, the two of them had several discussions about the inevitable mechanics of death and dying. One thing Eleanor made very clear was that she never wanted to be kept alive by life support or any other artificial means, and Lauren promised she would never let that happen.

Eleanor seemed to be in fairly good health when Lauren left for a trip overseas, so there was no way she could have anticipated that almost before her plane had taken off, her mother had collapsed and been rushed to intensive care, unconscious. Unable to reach Lauren, the hospital contacted her brother, Jay, who got there as quickly as he could from his home halfway across the country. Jay loved his mother as much as Lauren did and, unaware of the pact Lauren and Eleanor had made, desperately agreed to the option of life support when it seemed to be the only hope of saving her. By the time Lauren was able to catch an emergency flight home, Eleanor was gone, after spending her last twenty-four hours on earth unconscious, with her body being kept alive by nothing but a battery of machines.

"I don't blame Jay," Lauren told me. "He had no way of knowing how Mom felt about life support. But I knew. I promised her I would never let that happen. I broke the last promise I ever made to her, and I'm so afraid she'll never forgive me."

I had the benefit of Eleanor being right there with us, happy and healthy from The Other Side and thrilled at this opportunity to communicate to her daughter through me how much she adored her and how forgiveness isn't even an issue at Home, where the very air we breathe is permeated with the eternal, unconditional love of God. But even if Eleanor hadn't been able to join us at that particular moment, I could have promised Lauren the same thing I can promise everyone who's struggling with the same painful fear of unfinished business with loved ones who have passed on: Not only is it impossible for spirits to harbor the idea that we did anything wrong because there *is* no right or wrong on The Other Side, but they also completely understand us, watch over us, and treasure us with a depth and purity only possible in paradise.

Remember, pain, hurt, resentment, mistreatment, judgmentalism, worry, fear, and all other forms of negativity are human-made, not God-made, earthly realities. They literally don't exist at Home on The Other Side, which is precisely why we choose to come here from time to time—it's the only place where our spirits can have the first-hand experience of learning and growing through difficulty. Once we've made the transition from here to there, we're blessed with total recall of every moment of every life we've had, on earth and at Home, and every lesson we've learned from those lives. Knowledge and perspective come flooding back in a rush of understanding. We have complete access to all our charts from all our lives, and to everyone else's charts as well, so that we're fully, gratefully, compassionately aware of our purpose in their lives and their purpose in ours. With objective, ego-free insight into each act and each motive that has contributed to the whole of who we are as we thrive in God's immediate presence on The Other Side, forgiveness doesn't exist because *blame doesn't exist,* only love, as eternal and unconditional as the Father who created us all and started our spirits on this amazing journey to begin with.

Forgiveness from God

If you never believe anything else I ever say to you, believe this: God is not mean, vengeful, judgmental, or punishing. He is divine, glorious, all knowing, the Source of perfect goodness, comfort, joy, and infinite love. In His perfection there is no anger or disappointment, blame or disapproval. Those negatives, like all negatives, are human made, not God made. So when you pray to Him to forgive you, change it to a more accurate prayer that He will help you forgive yourself. And when you put the forgiveness of someone else in His hands, acknowledge at the same time that you're not praying for God's vengeance, which is impossible, but simply peace, to the very depth of your soul, that only He can provide.

The Exercise

As the white light of the Holy Spirit glows around you, silken bands of other colors descend to weave themselves into the drape of white . . . gold, the light of your Messiah . . . purple, the majestic light of God . . . rose, a soft deep red, the light of Azna, the Mother God . . .

One by one, the colors of light penetrate you, spiraling deep into your being, cleansing and healing every cell of your body, searching out the pain of every hurt that's ever been inflicted on you, every hurt you've ever inflicted that you've done your best to make right. The beautiful rose of Azna's light, the magnificent purple of God's light, the Messiah's rich gold light, the pure white of the light of the Holy Spirit, blend into one gentle, swirling spiral, finding, lifting out, and rinsing away the obstructions of old resentments, old grudges, old unresolved conflicts, a glowing whirlpool of color transforming anger into peace, bitterness into compassion.

And where the unforgivable still lingers, too dark a stain, God's purple light lingers, growing hot, persistent, roiling with power. Let the darkness go, release the stain into that purple light, giving the unforgivable to God. Let Him be the forgiver, so that you can be free and healed. The dark stain of the unforgivable is gone now, absorbed into infinite Wisdom, and in its place a fresh sense of relief, an exhale of the spirit, its tense anger washed away, making room for new growth.

God's light, still hot with power, blends with the others again and together the white, the gold, the purple, the rose, surge through your body and into your hands. You hold very still, feeling every cell, every muscle, of your hands fill with healing heat, healing so potent that everyone you touch, everyone who brushes against you, will be made more peaceful, more ready to forgive and to be forgiven.

Feel your hands become even warmer. Feel them pulsate. Know that you've been given the power to cleanse all resentment you carry and heal yourself with your own blessed, quiet touch. Through the glowing heat of white, gold, purple, and rose, you renew the promise you made to God when you came here, that this world will be finer, more compassionate, more committed to integrity and the dignity of the spirit than you found it, so that earth can become more like the Home you yearn for and will return to with joy someday, where kindness is as infinite as life itself and forgiveness, like the pain that demands it, is just a distant, meaningless memory.

As the white light of the Holy Spirit, the gold light of the Messiah, the purple light of God, and the rose light of Azna surge on through your body, healing your heart and magnifying your soul, let it become a glow that emanates from deep inside you, so that from this moment on you become a beacon of hope, release, mercy, and grace for all to see. Ask this in the name of the Father God, the Mother God, the blessed Messiah, and the Holy Spirit, and be strengthened by their love as you slowly open your eyes.

THE AFFIRMATION

"I will never again let my spirit be paralyzed and imprisoned by resentment. I will be as quick and compassionate to forgive as I wish to be forgiven. What I cannot forgive I will release into God's hands and move on, because as His child it is my divine right to grow and be free."

6

Joy

I'm sure it seems as irritating to you as it sometimes does to me that we have to work at it to find joy in our lives, while sadness and hard times are only too happy to leap out at us at the drop of a hat. Logically, it makes all the sense in the world. We chose to come here for the growth and education of our spirits, and as my Spirit Guide, Francine, has pointed out more than once when I've complained to her about life being tougher than I think I can handle, "What have you learned when things were good?" But emotionally, wouldn't it be nice, just every once in a while, if joy were as easily accessible as disappointment?

The fact is, we all did write some flashes of joy into our charts, if only to remind ourselves of Home, where joy is constant and eternal. What's tough is being willing to put out the effort to find it, staying out of our own way while we search for it, and then savoring it when we've got it, instead of immediately bracing ourselves for that moment when it will disappear again.

I've read several lovely, well-intentioned books on the subject of joy. Some of them were beautifully written, and the philosophies in them were perfectly sound. The problem was, once I'd finished them I had an urge to call the author and say, "Okay, this is very nice, but what is it I'm supposed to do, exactly?" I'm an activist when it comes to happiness. I don't believe for one minute that we can achieve it just by sitting around thinking about it. God really does help those who help themselves, and one truth I've learned the hard way is that if it's been too long since I felt something I could truly describe as joy, it's pretty reliably my fault.

I want to make it clear right up front—I can't offer you a guaranteed pathway to discovering your joy. If I could, believe me, I would personally take you by the hand and lead you there myself. I can offer you some guaranteed guidelines to help you find that path, though, and some self-imposed obstacles to avoid along the way.

Worry

There's a wonderful old story in which God, concerned that so many of His children were unhappy, gathered in a circle the one hundred unhappiest people He could find and told them to list their ten worst problems on a piece of paper and throw their lists into the middle of the circle. They were then invited to choose a list of problems they'd rather have instead. In the end, each of those hundred people chose the list they'd written themselves.

Joy and worry can't coexist. It's that simple. In fact, a good definition of *joy* is "the absence of worry." And what makes us worry is not knowing the outcome of a situation we're going through. It's our nature to be curious, to solve mysteries, to want answers, to yearn for conclusions and closure, about everything from a loved one's illness to relationship problems to dilemmas at work or school, about *everything.* We want to hear the punch line to even the worst jokes, and we hate unfinished stories, whether they're interesting or not. So in a way, since our lives could be described as a series of jokes and stories, some better than others, it's our nature to feel anxious until we know how every joke and story of our life ends.

What we forget too easily is that thanks to the detailed charts we composed before we came here, *we've already written all those endings,* to all our jokes and stories, endings that best serve the lessons, goals, and purposes we left The Other Side to accomplish. We've heard a thousand times the cliché that "sooner or later, everything works out for the best." That happens to be true, because we designed it that way. It's just very difficult to remember that in the middle of a crisis, and frankly when I've heard it at the wrong time, while I'm really upset, I've had to fight an urge to smack whoever said it right in the mouth. But again, we can eliminate a lot of worry through the certainty that, in the long run, our spirit minds will always guide us toward a perfect conclusion.

And speaking of clichés, I used to hear "God helps those who help themselves" and "Let go and let God" and think, *Which is it?* On paper, those two adages seem to contradict each other—are we supposed to dig in and slave over our problems, or are we supposed to sit back, put our feet up, and let God deal with them? It did finally come to me that those truisms are really the two brilliantly simple steps toward getting away from the habit of worrying, which will always be the biggest obstacle standing between us and joy. First, no matter what the situation, we owe it to ourselves to do everything we know to do toward the solution we're after. Then, once we're satisfied that there really is nothing more we can do, we need to stand back, stay out of the way, and let things finish unfolding as we, with God's guidance, charted them.

One of the most literal and admirable examples of "Do all you can, then let go and let God" was a client appropriately named Hope. She was deeply in love and planning a future with Victor, who'd been divorced for more than a year and had full custody of the three young children from that marriage. But out of nowhere Victor's ex-wife showed up, wanting to reconcile, using the children as an excuse when the truth was that the boyfriend she'd left Victor for had dumped her. The thought of his children having their mother with them again, and the romantic notion of second chances, allowed him to be talked into letting his ex-wife move back home, but he still loved Hope and wanted to be with her. In their last conversation before our reading, Hope told him that she loved him, and would miss him, but that she didn't want to hear from him again until he was ready to make a loving commitment, either to her or his ex-wife, because she wasn't interested in having only part of his heart. A smart woman, obviously, who respected herself enough to demand respect from him. She was also human, though, and very worried about how Victor and his ex-wife were getting along, whether or not he would come back to her, and if she should give in to her occasionally urgent temptation to call him or "happen to" run into him. I only asked her one question: "Is there anything you've left undone or unsaid between the two of you?" She thought about it and finally said no. Now, admittedly, I could probably have handled this one without being psychic, just from the countless times Montel has pointed out that "an ex is an ex for a reason." But I had the added bonus of being able to read her chart, and told her, "If you want him back temporarily, you can guilt him into it by calling him and telling him how miserable you are without him, which is exactly the trick his ex-wife pulled. If you want him back permanently and for the right reasons, you'll have him in six months, but only if you leave him alone completely, stay busy with your own life, let him get her out of his system once and for all, and, most important, let him experience the void in his life when you're not in it." In other words, let go and let God. By her own admission, she wasn't too good at doing nothing, but once I convinced her that sometimes, as in this case, doing nothing is doing *something,* she left my office with "Let go and let God" written on a piece of paper to keep beside her phone when the temptation hit again in the months to come. Hope did indeed leave Victor alone and did something by doing nothing, and I was wrong—he didn't come back to her in six months. It took four and a half.

I'm not telling you anything new when I say that worrying doesn't just stand between us and our full potential for the joy we've planned for ourselves, but it also accomplishes absolutely nothing. And believe me, I know firsthand what a hard habit it is to break. But I've made breaking it a priority in the last few years, and I'm getting there, by working toward the habit of taking the three steps I've just described whenever the temptation to worry hits:

- *Remember that worry is really your fear of not knowing the end of the story or situation you're in the middle of. But the truth is, you've already written that ending, one that will ultimately benefit you and help you reach your greatest good.*
- *Satisfy yourself that you've done everything you can productively do toward the happy ending we all hope for.*
- *Then let go and let God.*

The story I started this section with inspired me to try an exercise that I promise you is another good way to help break the habit of worrying, and, simple as it is, it will also teach you more about yourself than you might think.

Sit in a quiet place with pen and paper, and make a list of everything you're worried about, from the significant to the trivial. Be honest and thorough, and don't stop until your list is complete. Seal the list in an envelope and write the date on the envelope. Then surround the envelope with the white light of the Holy Spirit and pray, "Dear God, please let the contents of this envelope be resolved into Your divine white light of peace, through the efforts of my willing hands, guided by Your love and infinite wisdom. Amen." Now, put the sealed envelope in a safe, private, out-of-the-way place where you won't see it and be reminded of it but will be able to find it when the time comes, and make a note on your calendar to open the envelope again in exactly six months.

Take it from someone who uses this exercise, you'll be surprised at how many situations on that list worked themselves out on their own and, beyond that, how many you can't even remember having worried about at all. And the more you make this exercise a habit, the less of a habit worrying will be, which will bring you one step closer to the joy you deserve.

Live What You Believe

"Live what you believe" sounds almost too obvious to mention. The immediate impulse is to reply, "Who doesn't do that?" and move on to the next section. But when you really start thinking about it, I bet you'll find that very few people you know actually live what they believe, and because they don't, they cause themselves a lot of unnecessary conflict and throw even more obstacles in the path that leads to the potential joy in their lives.

We don't just come here with knowledge from our past lives and our lives on The Other Side, we also come here with deeply rooted beliefs that lie at the heart of the charts we've written for this lifetime. Sadly, the noise of earth, the behavior around us, and the dogma that gets thrown at us as "truth" can overshadow those beliefs if we're not careful to listen closely to our own spirits, our Spirit Guides, and the whispers of Angels' wings and centuries of loved ones' voices from Home. When what we do is out of synch with what we believe, that means we're not on track with our chart, and being off the track of our chart is guaranteed to make joy just another one of those lovely sounding experiences that happen to everyone else but us.

The quickest, easiest way to determine if we're living what we believe is to list the details of our behavior and our life—each one of which we chose, whether we like admitting that or not—and then put the words *I believe* in front of each statement. Here are a few examples that are more common than they should be, just to give you the general idea:

- *I believe* if I attend my church/temple/synagogue on a weekly basis, I can claim to be a fine, religious person, no matter how prejudiced, dishonest, rude, abusive, inhumane, greedy, or uncharitable I might be for the rest of the week.
- *I believe* it's logical to treat my spouse and other loved ones like dirt but then punish my children when they're disrespectful.

- *I believe* it's perfectly fine to talk badly about my friends behind their backs.
- *I believe* if I betray the trust of those who love me, it's acceptable as long as they don't find out about it or I can lie my way out of it.
- *I believe* it's okay to break the law from time to time if I feel like it, especially if it's a "little" crime like shoplifting or drinking a beer with my fourteen-year-old.
- *I believe* I have the right to turn my back on my children if something or someone more interesting and less demanding comes along.

Well, you get the gist. Living what you believe can be examined by taking a long look at the probability that those around you use what you do to conclude what your beliefs are, and it's not always accurate, something to be proud of, or even very attractive. But, *please,* in the pursuit of that rare and exquisite thing called joy, wherever your beliefs are finer than the ways in which you're treating yourself and those around you, it's never too late to elevate yourself to be a walking testament to everything you know in your God-center to be right and true. Living what you believe puts you back in step with the purpose you designed in the chart you wrote, and that in itself will bring joy to your sacred, Homesick spirit.

Postponing Joy

We've all fallen into this trap at some time or other—saying either silently or out loud, "I'll be happy when . . ." or, "I won't be happy until . . ." It's another bad habit, making our joy conditional on some future event, as if nothing else but that one event could possibly satisfy our pursuit of happiness. And ironically, by the time that "when" or that "until" comes around, either it's not as life altering as we expected it to be, or we have a new set of problems that almost overshadow the "when" or "until" to the point where we barely notice them.

The reasons we tend to postpone joy are almost as interesting as the fact that we do it. After all, logically, why would we habitually put off something we claim to want so much?

One reason is that, believe it or not, a lot of people are actually afraid to feel a moment of joy, because they're so afraid of that moment when it will be gone. It's not unlike being frightened of heights because there's so much farther to fall than if we just stay at ground level. It's sad how common it is to find comfort in problems and disappointment to the point of looking for them, clinging to them, and prolonging them, for no other reason than that there's a false sense of safety in the familiarity of hard times. I've had more clients than I care to remember who were much more receptive to any bad news I had to give them than to the good news available to them in the future if they wouldn't ambush themselves before they got there. It's the emotional version of living in a corner of your basement in case a tornado hits. Yes, you might feel more secure there, and, yes, you'll probably survive the unlikely event of a tornado, but, my God, what a tragedy to deny yourself just one glorious day in the sun.

There's also a tendency to postpone joy because we get confused about where we're supposed to find it, so it ends up seeming easier to put off the search until some other day, if not to simply give up entirely. We hear about it, we're given reason to believe that other people have access to it, and we assume incorrectly that they know something we don't or that they're luckier than we are—we just need that one lottery ticket, that one career break, that one relationship, that one great car or fabulous piece of jewelry, that one glimpse of fame, that one dream house, and we'll be as joyful as they are. I'm not going to carry on at length about something you've already heard a million times, that some of the unhappiest people I know have every one of those things and have discovered that there's not a rose in the world that doesn't come with thorns. But what I do want to stress, because it's the truth, is that the only waste of time in the search of joy is to look for it "out there." It lies inside us, waiting for us to notice it. It lies in our own God-center, in our wise, eternal soul which knows that joy is not a circumstance. Joy is a moment, no matter how brief, when we're so in synch with our chart and our divine Father that, for those few heartbeats, we wouldn't trade places with anyone else on earth.

We have a tradition in our family that helps us watch for those moments of joy together and point them out, and I'm thrilled that it's become as much of a habit among my grandchildren as it is among us adults, because it's a habit that will stay with them all their lives. It was originally inspired by the existence of the Scanning Machine. The Scanning Machine is one of our first stops on The Other Side, and in it we view, in three-dimensional hologram form, each and every instant of our lives and, if we like, the lives of our loved ones as well. Bearing that eventuality in mind, whenever there is a glimpse of joy, some freeze-frame of a perfect sight or feeling that we wouldn't have missed for anything, no matter how significant or trivial, one of us is guaranteed to say, "Flag this." The translation of *flag this* is "Here's something we want to linger over at the Scanning Machine."

As I said at the beginning of this book, I am very blessed, with an exciting life many people might envy (if they didn't inspect it too closely). But I'll tell you the most recent flag-this moment: my seven-year-old grand-daughter Angelia, surrounded by her beloved menagerie of puppies, completely absorbed in a crafts project, inexplicably dressed in her little leotard, tutu, and swimming goggles. She didn't notice my son Chris and me when we rounded the corner and spotted her, she just kept right on busily working as we stared in enchanted amazement, and Chris got out a whispered "Flag this," just as I was opening my mouth to say it. A successful career, best-selling books, travel throughout the world—but at that silly, supposedly trivial sight I felt a swelling of pure, absolute joy and almost envied myself, if that makes sense, for being graced enough not to have missed it. In fact, when you're on The Other Side at the Scanning Machine, consider this your invitation to scan my life and jump right to the flagged moments. Most of them will be no more significant than that, and none of them will be more treasured.

As you start each new day, promise yourself to watch for every event or feeling you want to flag to relive and cherish someday at the Scanning Machine. Keep a journal of them if you like—whatever it takes to start the habit of anticipating joy, not disappointment, not "when" or "until," but right now, today, inside of you, where the God-center of your joyful spirit lies waiting for you to notice.

Give What You're Deprived Of

I recently met a client who decided that, rather than getting a reading, she'd prefer to spend our time together listening to herself talk about how bleak and unfulfilling and unfair her life was. When I was finally able to get a word in edgewise, I gave her the give-what-you're-deprived-of advice, to which she impatiently snapped, "What I'm deprived of is money. How am I supposed to give money if I don't have any?" Believe me, with her negativity and determination to be a victim, I knew that money was the least of what was lacking in her life. But since she wasn't about to let me help her, and since I had a waiting room full of clients who might actually be there to accomplish something, I stood, handed her back the fee she'd given me, and said, "There. Now you have money. See how fast that works?" She was still in shock as I escorted her out the door.

You'll never hear me claim that money isn't important, but when I think about the times of real joy in my life, I realize that money had nothing to do with them. The point I was trying to make with that misery-addicted client is about those voids in life that, when they're filled, really can nourish our spirits with the joy they're hungry for.

And if, by the way, your first response to "giving what you're deprived of" is "Why should I give anything, when no one ever gives anything to me?" let me simply point out that it's that exact attitude that creates deprivation in the first place. If every one of us would declare that question off limits for just one short month, I swear to you we'd see such a remarkable change in this world that we'd eventually be able to eliminate the word *deprivation* from the dictionary.

Giving what you're deprived of is very simple. It requires some thought and a bit of effort, but thought and effort can be rewarding enough all by themselves to be worth the time they take. Best of all, it works, because it's an active expression of the universal truth of karma, or balance of experience, or "What goes around comes around," or whichever way of wording that perfect, inarguable principle is most comfortable for you. Here are just a few examples:

If you need a friend, be a friend. I promise,

someone you know right now needs someone they can trust, someone to talk to,
someone's shoulder to cry on, someone to
laugh with. Be that friend for them.

If you're lonely, end someone's loneliness.
There's a hospital or nursing home or children's shelter near you, and there's someone in it who never has a visitor, never has
anyone who stops by to say hello without
getting paid for it, never receives a greeting
card or a freshly picked flower or a book to
read or a toy to play with. Be that visitor for
them.

If you're hungry, feed someone. Every
time you're at the grocery store, spend one
extra dollar for a can of soup or a package
of cookies or some other item with a long
shelf life and set it aside. And then, once a
month, anonymously deliver that food
you've gathered to a nearby shelter, a family
you know of that's down on its luck, a rescue mission, the shut-in down the street, or
a worthy charity like the Red Cross or the
Salvation Army. The hungrier we are, the
harder it can get to believe in Angels. Be
someone's Angel.

If you're grieving, comfort someone. At
your church, in your neighborhood, in some

grief support group not far away, through your local television or radio news station, or even on the Internet, there's someone who's suffering from the same singular, aching pain of loss you are and needs to be held and assured by someone who understands that they don't have to go through it alone. Be that comfort for them.

Again, you get the idea. Anyone who already practices "giving what you're deprived of" will back me up on the fact that there is no joy quite like filling the void in someone else's life that you've been feeling in yours. No one but you even needs to know that your motives are selfish and that what you end up getting back will be ten times what you've given. That can be your own private, joyful secret.

Pick a Dream, Any Dream

One of my most unforgettable clients was a sparkling sixty-eight-year-old woman named Elizabeth. She was about to take an extended trip to Africa and wanted to be sure her children and grandchildren would be okay while she was gone. I couldn't keep the delight out of my voice when I realized and said, "You're going to Egypt. To *work.*" She grinned ear to ear. It seems she had just received her college degree in archaeology and so impressed her professor that he invited her on a dig he'd been planning for six years. "I've been fascinated by archaeology since I was a child. I don't know why," she told me. "I do," I said. "That's your occupation on The Other Side." That didn't surprise her at all. She went on to say that at the time she graduated from high school, there was no money for her to go to college to pursue her passion. "Besides, my parents told me I wasn't smart enough for college, I'd just be wasting my time. My late husband must have told me a thousand times that a woman's place was in the home. And my children and grandchildren have been telling me for years that I'm too old for all this." I asked her how she managed not to let all of that negative input discourage her. She winked and said, "Easy. I didn't believe them." I still have the postcard she sent me from Egypt two months later, where she was having the time of her life.

Elizabeth was a brilliant example of refusing to accept negative input, which I call "determinism." Determinism is that ridiculous list of purported "truths" about ourselves that a few careless people use to try to limit our self-confidence and *predetermine* our failure. "You're not smart enough," "Your place is in the home," and "You're too old" define determinism beautifully, as do some of the "facts" my mother used to tell me about myself, including my personal favorite, "Face it, Sylvia, you'll never have a career."

More importantly, Elizabeth was also a brilliant example of the utter joy to be found in making a dream come true—she was honestly one of the most joyful, inspiring people I've ever met. It's in her honor that I offer the last exercise of this chapter, just one more giant but simple step on the path toward that joy I so wish for you.

The Exercise

I want you to write down every bit of determinism you've ever been told or ever told yourself, anything and everything that, as you sit there today, makes you feel unable, limited, less than, and incapable. Then, take that list, shred it, and throw it into the near-

est garbage can where it belongs, while you remind yourself silently or out loud, "Sorry, I'm not buying it anymore. I was created by God, and God doesn't make junk.."

Now, rid of that determinism nonsense, I want you to list every dream you've ever dreamed for yourself, from as far back as you can remember. It doesn't matter how big or small or silly or unlikely they seem, just write them down without judging them, whether it was becoming an astronaut or learning to grow a healthy African violet (water them from the bottom, don't get their leaves wet, and add a drop of dishwashing liquid to their water) or taking dog-grooming lessons or reading the entire works of Shakespeare. Cross off the ones that no longer interest you and add any new ones that occur to you as you go along. Once your list is complete—please, I swear to you you'll thank me later—choose the one that seems the most accessible and go after it with every ounce of passion in you. Don't you dare give up until you've satisfied that dream, then return to your list, draw a star beside it, and choose the most accessible of those remaining to go after next. Whether you end up with one star or a whole page full of them, be proud of what you accomplished, thank yourself for the realized dream, and, above all, celebrate to the core of your spirit the exquisite joy of knowing you loved yourself and the God-center inside you enough to try.

THE AFFIRMATION

"I feel the golden light from my Father God shining on me, a gift of His perpetual, unconditional love, for which I will thank Him from this day forward by pursuing and sharing the joy I knew before and will know again in His presence on The Other Side when my purpose here is finished."

7

Guilt

Guilt is a complicated and incredibly powerful force. A little guilt is healthy. Too much
guilt is destructive. The absence of guilt is
spiritually disastrous. Guilt can impel criminals to compulsively talk about their crimes,
and the innocent but mentally ill to confess
to felonies they never committed. Even
those who theoretically "got away with it"
become self-destructive or commit suicide.
Some religions rely more on guilt than on
faith for their success, many relationships
survive on guilt long after love has vanished,
and as manipulation tactics go, it's without
a doubt among the two or three most popular. As grateful as we should be that we're

capable of feeling it, we should be even more diligent about learning to get rid of it. If there's any other emotion on earth that shares those qualities, I can't imagine what it is.

I do want to get one special category of humans who feel no guilt out of the way so that I can spend the majority of this chapter focused on the rest of us. I have to brace myself for this, because every time Lindsay and I write about these people we're subjected to their protests in the form of negative energy, from inexplicable static that makes our taped discussions of them inaudible to their shutting off the electricity, but only in the room we're working in. Just as most of us can powerfully project light, this group can powerfully project darkness, which is why they're known as the Dark Side.

The Absence of Guilt

The Dark Side are the only people among us who never have and never will experience guilt, let alone any other genuine human emotion. In psychiatric terms, they're sociopaths and psychopaths, remorseless, amoral, devoid of a conscience, untreatable, insidious, and immune to any efforts at rehabilitation, since it's impossible to rehabilitate anyone whose only motive is to incapacitate any light that crosses their path. Darkness, after all, can't exist where there's light, and that fact drives the Dark Side's lives more than any other.

If you've heard or read my loathing of the Dark Side, also known as "dark entities," you can probably say this right along with me, and I hope you can, because it's so important: *God is not to blame for the existence of the Dark Side.* Dark entities are Godless, not because God created them that way or because He turned away from them, but because they made a conscious decision to turn away from Him, in this or some past lifetime. If you've ever loved someone who ignored you, or refused to acknowledge that you even exist, you understand the relationship between God and the Dark Side.

It would be so nice to tell you that dark entities are uncommon, or that there's an easy way to spot them the moment you meet them. Sadly, though, it's probable that you have one in your life right now, or that you're just trying to recover from one and are still trying to figure out where you went wrong. Dark entities are rarely sneering, moustache-twirling monsters with beady eyes and an evil laugh. Only a small fraction of them are in prison right now, and only a minority of them even have criminal records, because so much of their destruction is spiritual but, sadly, not illegal. In fact, since they can't hurt you, physically or emotionally, until they're close to you, the Dark Side can be some of the most charming people you'll ever meet when you're first getting to know them, and you might find it uncanny how much they have in common with you. You're not apt to notice for a while that they took all their cues from you about how incredibly alike the two of you are. Only when they've secured your trust and you've let down your guard will they begin to reveal that they're really not much more than very gifted mimics, duplicating human behavior without ever feeling it and capable of brutal coldness, cruelty, deviousness, and abuse, all designed to make you feel utterly powerless and, more to the point, extinguish your light to help spread their darkness a little farther.

There are two common mistakes we light

entities make when we realize we've let a dark entity get close to us. One is that we remember so fondly and longingly how sweet, sensitive, and attentive they were at the beginning that we trick ourselves into thinking if we just behave well and shower them with love, we can inspire that loving behavior out of them again. The reality is, that loving behavior was nothing but a brilliant performance to gain our attention and proximity, and they'll only trot it out onstage again if they start to think we might be getting ready to catch on to their game and walk away. The other mistake is to fall into the trap of believing that it is our mission, as spiritual, God-centered people, to understand them, change them, and ultimately save them from themselves. Take it from someone who's tried more than once to rescue a dark entity and almost got destroyed in the process, don't waste one more minute of your time, your energy, your well-meaning spirit, or your kind heart. Do as Christ told us: "Shake the dust off your feet and walk away." It's not that the Dark Side is more powerful than we are. *They're not.* It's just that in order to beat them at their own game, we would have to abandon God, our faith, and our conscience, which would make us exactly like them, and then, guess what—they've won anyway.

Don't worry, they do get theirs in the end. Instead of going Home to the blessed paradise among our loved ones, Spirit Guides, Angels, and messiahs in the divine presence of God on The Other Side when this lifetime ends, they go through a place called the Left Door and right back in utero again to start another life without having learned a thing.

I recently heard an interview with Mark Klaas, whose young daughter Polly was brutally, horribly murdered by a man I won't dignify by putting his name in print. Mark Klaas was asked if he forgave this man. He said, "No, that will never happen. And I'm sure he would scoff at my forgiveness anyway."

I'm sure he would too. And that's the best description of the Dark Side's absence of guilt I've heard in a very long time.

Dealing with Guilt

Now that we've learned to be thankful that we're capable of feeling guilty, we can explore the unfortunate fact that most of us feel it far more often than we should or need to. I do mean "we," too, believe me. I don't remember the last time I boarded a plane for a lecture tour without feeling like the lowest creature on earth as my grandchildren's heart-wrenching cries of "No, Bagdah, please don't leave us!" echoed in my ears. You'd think I didn't know that they're invariably giggling, swimming, playing, and romping with their menageries of pets again before my flight even takes off. Come to think of it, speaking of that menagerie, I don't even escape guilt free when I leave the dogs at the groomer's and see that pitiful look in their eyes, accusing me of everything from abandonment to betrayal.

But even I really do know that ultimately I'd feel a whole lot guiltier, and rightly so, if I didn't take good care of our pets, and if I gave my grandchildren the message that commitments and responsibilities are so unimportant that they can be dropped at the slightest whimper.

The guilt we all experience from time to time that's much harder to deal with is the guilt of a lost or careless moment, something we did or didn't do, something said or unsaid, that leaves a lingering pain which, like all emotional pain, has an inevitable impact and consequence somewhere, somehow. And while the ability to feel guilt is healthy, seeking guilt out, embracing it, and leaving it unresolved are like tying an anvil to our spirit, locking our life into a cell made of hurt, where no sun can come in, and the irony is, we're the only ones with the key to let ourselves out.

Remember, we're on this earth for one reason: to learn lessons for the progress of our soul, as part of our commitment to God. Every bit of unresolved guilt we carry with us is another unlearned lesson, and we can't move on to new lessons until we've conquered the ones we're already faced with. So developing the skill of releasing both warranted and unwarranted guilt isn't just helpful, it's essential to our spirit's success in this lifetime.

The difference between warranted and unwarranted guilt can be summarized in one word: *motive.* If whatever you're feeling guilty about is something you knew would cause someone pain, but out of greed, jealousy, selfishness, or sheer meanness you went ahead with it anyway, then you *should* feel guilty. You *are* guilty. And as we discussed in the "Forgiveness" chapter, you can learn from the experience by stepping up to it and making progress because of it, or you can hide from it, deny it, blame anyone but yourself, and count on repeating the same mistake over and over again.

On the other hand, if you're feeling guilty about something in which your motive was pure and harmless, and any pain that resulted was unintentional, for God's sake, and yours, let yourself off the hook and put it behind you. I found a simple way to help myself do that, although it took me some time to get into the habit of it, and it can help you, too, if you'll make yourself do it and stay at it.

The first time I consciously tried this technique was a few years ago, in the hospital where my father died. Daddy had been ill for a while, and I knew our time together here was coming to an end. I had been at his bedside nonstop for days when I decided to step out of the room for a moment to get a drink of water. In that moment when I was gone and he was alone, Daddy passed away. My guilt was almost as crushing as my grief at losing this amazing, magical man who had always been as much my best friend as my funny, devoted, loving father. I couldn't have waited five more minutes to leave that room? The person closer to him than anyone else in his life, and I wasn't beside him as he took his last breath? A supposed world-renowned psychic, and I couldn't even sense that my timing on that of all occasions couldn't have been worse? Somewhere in the middle of that barrage of self-torture, I managed to subconsciously remember a tip my Spirit Guide, Francine, had given me once on a different subject, and from the depth of my soul I suddenly and silently screamed the word "Stop!" loudly enough to drown out all those absurd, unanswerable questions, to replace them with more logical, more truthful ones. Did I mean to leave Daddy's bedside at the exact moment he was going to die? Of course not. Had I known that moment had arrived, would I have waited? Of course. Would Daddy, who was as sure of my stubbornness as he was of my profound love for him, understand that as horrible as my timing was, it was also an accident? There wasn't a doubt in my mind about that. In the years since, I've taken a few tentative steps down that same road of guilt about Daddy's death again, but that loud, silent

"Stop!" is getting more effective every time I use it.

The "Stop!" technique has also worked well for many of my clients who are carrying around unwarranted guilt. One in particular was Tracy, who was also an example of how guilt can be used as a cruel means of manipulation if we let ourselves buy into it. Tracy's mother, Helen, was, to put it politely, a miserable human being I wouldn't wish on my worst enemy. Tracy's father had abandoned his wife and daughter when Tracy was two years old, and frankly, if there hadn't been a child involved, I might have been tempted to wonder what took him so long. Helen decided to hold Tracy responsible for her husband's departure and essentially held Tracy hostage for it for the rest of her mean-spirited life. As far as Helen was concerned, Tracy owed her a debt she could never repay, and no matter what Tracy did for her mother, it never was and never would be enough. Tracy, a successful career woman, rented a modest apartment for herself so that she could afford to buy Helen a lavish condominium, which Helen complained about from the day she moved in. Tracy leased Helen a new car every two years, but they were never good enough, or big enough, or small enough, or fast enough, or slow enough, or red enough, or blue enough. Tracy even estranged a lot of her friends by including Helen in most of her social plans, only to discover that Helen was an equal opportunity abuser, not happy until she'd offended and alienated everyone in the room. As her coup de grâce, she surprised Tracy one day with an offer to prepare a lovely dinner to celebrate Tracy's birthday. Tracy arrived at the condo right on time, wine and flowers in hand, to find Helen dead of the most apparent suicide she could think to devise.

It's an understatement to say that Tracy's main issue was guilt when she walked into my office two months after her mother's suicide, although what she thought she wanted me to tell her was that her mother was finally at peace on The Other Side. I couldn't do that. The good news was, Helen wasn't earthbound, so at least she was really out of Tracy's life once and for all. The bad news for some poor unsuspecting woman was that Helen was already in utero again, and God help the family who's trying to deal with her now and undoubtedly wondering where they went wrong. But Tracy, who'd been fed a steady diet of guilt her whole life and didn't even recognize it as a choice, was still agonizing over why she couldn't seem to make her mother happy, why she couldn't have prevented her mother's suicide—and, she finally admitted, what kind of monster she must be that, in her most private moments, she was actually a little relieved that her mother was gone. I'll never forget the shock on her face when I said, "My mother was a dark entity too. We're relieved that they're gone because we're not masochists. As my Spirit Guide always says, 'You only have to honor thy father and mother if they're *honorable.*' " Tracy told me later that it was the first time she'd laughed in longer than she could remember, and the first time in her life she'd ever laughed about her mother.

At any rate, in addition to giving Tracy the exercise you'll find at the end of this chapter, I also shared the simple technique of saying, "Stop!" every time she gave herself anything but credit and high praise for the devotion she'd shown to a woman nine other people out of ten would have bailed out on decades earlier. She promised to try it, she became very adept at it, and I was thrilled to get a card from her a few months ago telling me that she's just adopted a baby and is determined to be the most caring, giving, loving single mother any child ever had. Knowing how much better a mother I am by simply taking my mother's example and doing exactly the opposite, I don't doubt it for a minute.

If you're struggling with guilt when you truly know you did the very best you could in a given situation and meant no harm, yell, "Stop!" the instant so much as a word of self-doubt enters your mind. You'll be pleasantly surprised at how quickly you'll break the unwarranted guilt habit, if only because you're so tired of hearing yourself yell, "Stop!"

Revenge

Frustrating as this may be to hear, revenge is one of the most time-wasting, self-destructive sources of guilt you can possibly indulge in. In fact, you may have already read my favorite quote on the subject of revenge, an ancient Chinese saying that goes, "When you seek revenge, you might as well dig two graves—one for the other person and one for yourself."

Believe me, I know just exactly how

tempting the idea of revenge can be. In sixty-four years, most of them very public, I've been on the receiving end of my share of hurt, betrayal, and dirty tricks, and I've fantasized a lot of clever, sometimes diabolical, ways of getting even. Of course, the truth is, when we've been wronged and done nothing to deserve it, we're *already* even. It's the person who wronged us who's got karma to deal with, and I'll pass on deliberately wishing that on myself, thank you.

One of the most idiotic aspects of revenge is that it demands devoting a lot of time and energy to the person who wronged us, when they're inevitably the last person on earth who deserves even a glance from us in their direction. And it's entirely possible that that person will interpret any attention from us, either positive or negative, as flattering. Do we really want to add insult to injury by complimenting someone who treated us badly?

On a practical level, it's simply a fact that many popular forms of revenge are just plain against the law, and any attorney will back me up when I promise you that "I was upset" and/or "He/she deserved it" are not defenses that will hold up in court. Client after client has sat in my office trying to recover not only from the initial wrong that was done to them but also from the legal, financial, and guilt consequences of some lame, impulsive effort to avenge that wrong. Instead of feeling satisfied, they invariably feel like fools, being ordered by a judge to pay for tires they slashed, clothing they burned, the computer they trashed, or the harassment they indulged in, while the person they simply wanted revenge against gets to stand there looking like the victim in the eyes of the law. And nine out of ten of those clients have added, after telling me about some embarrassing stab at retribution, "I still can't believe I did it. I thought I was a better person than that, but now I feel as if I'm just as low as the person I was trying to get back at." Every one of them would agree with me, the guilt is almost always even more expensive than losing the property-damage or harassment lawsuit.

Never confuse the word revenge *with the word* justice. As strongly as I believe in not wasting time, effort, and potential prosecution on revenge, I'm an even more passionate believer in justice. I work with law enforcement officers, district attorneys, prosecutors, and defense attorneys all over the country in the interest of justice, and I'll continue that work for the rest of my life. While I might sympathize with clients who've found themselves in legal trouble from an impulsive act of revenge, I've never once said, "You shouldn't have to pay for breaking the law." In fact, my hair is still standing on end from a client I spent two hours with a while ago. He and his estranged wife are involved in a bitter custody battle, and out of sheer vengeance toward him, she's accused him of molesting their young daughter. There's no evidence, since it never happened, but the mere allegation is bound to stay with him, and with the child who's being coached to support her mother's claims. I said this to him, and I'll say it on paper—I would enthusiastically support a law in which, when it's proven that someone has knowingly falsely accused a person of a felony, the accuser should have to serve the same amount of time the accused would have served if they'd been convicted. At least I was able to assure my client that he'll end up with sole custody and a clear conscience, which is infinitely more than his estranged wife has to look forward to.

Spiritually, revenge is even less affordable than it is financially or legally, because it inevitably draws us into the other person's chart and therefore off track from our own. When we composed our chart, we wrote in our own mistakes and our own lessons to learn, toward the specific purposes we intended to accomplish while we're here. When someone wrongs us, it's their mistake and their lesson to learn, and the inevitability of karma and their chart guarantees that sooner or later, they *will* learn. When that lesson comes, it will be their problem to face, not ours. But if we seek revenge, we're essentially taking time out from our chart to concern ourselves with theirs, which is not unlike neglecting our own homework assignment and failing a course because we were so busy doing an enemy's homework instead.

And finally, with the exception of the Dark Side, we're all on this earth for the ultimate purpose of leaving it better than we found it, and to forward the progress of our spirits. There is no progress to be found in emulating and perpetuating hurtful behavior. There is only precious ground to be lost along our spirits' eternal path, more distance instead of less between us and our ultimate spiritual potential that we'll only have to make up for later.

Confession

One of the most compelling, comforting, and influential voices of my Catholic-school years was a Jesuit priest named Father Nadeau, who once said to me, among many other wise observations, "Sylvia, confession is good for only one soul—your own."

Granted, there are few more effective ways of getting rid of guilt than to simply sit down, bare our soul, and confess every wrong we've done. And in most situations, I'm absolutely in favor of confessing, taking responsibility for our actions, and backing up our promises to do better. But I know Father Nadeau would agree, as do several of my psychologist and psychiatrist friends, that too many people cross the line between honest confession and dumping their burdens in someone else's lap and then walking away feeling much better while that someone else is now stuck with all that added weight they never asked for, with no place to put it.

Twenty or thirty years ago we went

through a phase in this country in which it became fashionable to "own your feelings," to almost proudly proclaim every thought and feeling, every misstep and mistake, to blather endlessly and self-indulgently about everything we've ever done, all in the name of "truth," "openness," and "total exposure." Unfortunately, other critical considerations like compassion, discretion, privacy, and sensitivity took a beating in the process, and a lot of people relieved themselves of guilt at the expense of loved ones who were left with nothing but pain and more information than they ever needed or wanted or could do anything about.

The biggest key to the decision about whether or not to confess to a loved one is unselfishness. If what we're feeling guilty about is something they have a genuine right to know, we need to be unselfish enough and brave enough to tell them. If our only motive for confessing is that it will make us feel better, it's a selfish and unfair thing to do. And if you can't figure out which is which, *please* talk out the decision with a trusted friend, minister, priest, rabbi, psychologist, doctor, *legitimate* spiritual counselor, or other discreet, objective person who won't be emotionally affected by whatever you have to tell them, and let them help guide you toward the course of action that will be best for all concerned, not just for *ourselves.*

Two recent clients illustrated the difference perfectly. Client #1, married for ten years, had an affair with a man with whom she and her husband had a lot of friends in common. When rumors of the affair inevitably started, she didn't just deny it, she sat back and watched as her husband innocently and vehemently defended her honor. The truth came out, and he was devastated on several levels, having to deal with her betrayal, her lies, and the apologies he owed to the many people he'd yelled at for damaging his wife's reputation when it turned out that all they were doing was telling the truth. Should she have confessed to him when she began to realize she was seriously considering this affair? Without a doubt. Her selfishness in keeping her mouth shut did serious damage to countless lives, and she's now lost her husband, all those friends, who understandably sided with her faithful husband in this dispute, and, even though she had yet to fully realize it, every ounce of self-respect. Client #2, on the other hand, found himself in legal trouble. He owned up to it, hired a reputable attorney to help him through it, satisfied the fines and terms of his sentence, and has probably become the most law-abiding citizen you'll ever meet. He managed to keep every bit of what happened from his elderly parents, who live three thousand miles away but to whom he's always been very close. The whole experience was a nightmare for him, and all his life he's been honest with his parents and able to turn to them for unconditional emotional support. It would relieve his guilt considerably if he sat them down and told them about it, especially now that it's all behind him and there's nothing more to fear. Should he confess to them? Absolutely not. Other than making him feel better, what would dumping this news on them possibly accomplish, and what on earth would they be able to do with it, except ache for what he went through and wish they could have helped while he was going through it?

So again, before you confess, *think.* Keeping something from someone who needs to know is an act of selfishness. But so is confession for the sheer sake of shifting the weight of your burden to someone else, for no other reason than that you won't have to carry it anymore.

Sin

Finally, if you're feeling guilty because you've committed what "everyone" or the Bible defines as a "sin," *please* believe me: the word *sin* has come to be used as a part of religious and social dogma for no other purpose than to make us behave and to try to separate "good people" from "bad people," with no regard whatsoever for Christ's admonition to "judge not, lest ye be judged." When dogma becomes too much of a priority, it causes us to stop thinking logically, and even worse, it overpowers the faith that is supposed to be the real heart of every religion.

Sin means "missing the mark." It means we've let ourselves down and offended our own conscience. And that's *all* it means. It doesn't mean God is sitting there scowling at us and reaching for his imaginary list of punishments, it doesn't mean he loves us one bit less, and it certainly doesn't mean we're less worthy or important than any of His other children on earth.

If you're reaching for your Bible now to prove me wrong, and to point to things that you know it specifically says are sins, *period,* that's fine, as long as you don't just selectively scan it to find the verses that support your personal position. Read every word of it, from beginning to end, and then tell me that you believe it's meant to be taken literally, especially the Old Testament, and that every bit of it is a valid guideline for what's right and what's wrong, what's a sin and what's not.

Leviticus 18:22, for example, is a popular verse for people to point to as proof that homosexuality is "an abomination." But according to Leviticus 11:10, eating shellfish is an abomination too. Do you really believe that? Leviticus 21:17–21 makes it clear that we shouldn't approach the altar of God if we have a defect in our sight, which I guess lets me out, since I can't read without contacts or glasses. I'm in even worse trouble than that, though, according to Exodus 35:2, because apparently anyone who works on the Sabbath should be put to death, and I admit it, I sometimes do as many as twenty readings on Sunday to try to stay current with my waiting list. It's a good thing I never had a daughter, since Exodus 21:7 says I should sell her into slavery. But there have been times when my two sons have been "stubborn or rebellious," so I guess I need to take them to the outskirts of my village and have them stoned to death as Deuteronomy 21:18 strongly advocates.

No one loves the Bible more than I do. I've read all twenty-six versions, some of them many times. I guess that's why it makes my hair stand on end to see it used as an excuse for prejudice, bigotry, and judgmentalism, and why I'm ending this chapter on guilt with a reminder: We're here to learn, and in the course of learning, we've written plenty of mistakes into our charts. That's more than enough guilt for us to tackle and overcome without adding this misunderstood, highly selective sledgehammer called "sin" to the burden.

The Exercise

Surround yourself with the gold, purple, and white lights of God's protection and loving spirit until you feel those lights warming you, relaxing you, helping your breath become deep, rhythmic, and nourishing.

From where you're sitting, a white bridge slowly rises up and extends itself, welcoming and safe, over a sparkling, glowing, rushing white river. You rise from your chair, curious and eager to experience this magnificent span of white, and find a large sealed bag at your feet. You pick it up, straining at its weight, and its weight alone defines it for you as all the guilt you've been carrying that you've taken upon yourself, that's been slowing your steps along the path of your spirit's journey, making it so much harder than it needs to be.

Carrying the bag, still straining, you begin to walk toward the bridge, seeing the gold flecks in its railings and arches glittering and dancing in the bright sun. The instant your bare feet touch the cool, smooth, refreshing surface of the bridge floor, you feel strength surging through you, and your steps become confident and sure as your purpose on this bridge washes over you like a soft whisper of grace.

The heavy bag of dark, hurtful guilt is in your arms as you walk to the railing of the bridge and look down into the white, glis-

tening river below, a powerful rush of pure, cleansing, sacred love. A mist of its spray kisses your face, reassuring, an embrace of understanding and permission, and, your purpose growing stronger with each deep breath, you open this bag of emotional debris and lean just far enough over the railing to turn the bag upside down and empty it into the white water. As each dark guilt hits the surface, the water roils slightly and then consumes that darkness, just as all light consumes darkness, and you watch as this beautiful river, this flowing embodiment of the omnipotent Holy Spirit, absorbs and dissolves, one by one, each hasty word, each misstep, each unintended hurt you've been carrying for so long. You stand and watch until the bag is empty and useless, and you feel grateful tears in your eyes as you see that this blessed white river has accepted the heaviness in your spirit without being compromised or darkened, just as God so lovingly holds our imperfections in His arms without growing any less perfect Himself.

Your burden mercifully gone, you look for the first time to the far side of the bridge, where an emerald-green meadow dotted with a prism of wildflowers spreads like a soft carpet for as far as you can see. From the center of the meadow a small group of people start walking toward you. You stand watching, unsure, until they come closer and their faces come into focus, each one sad, each one a little afraid, but each one present, available, looking to you for some sign of whether or not it's worth their time to stay.

You recognize them now, these people with whom you need to make things right, people pushed away not by their choice but by your own guilt. And as you meet their eyes you know that only you can take away their sadness and their fear, because you're the one who caused it. For a moment you hesitate, wondering if you have the strength and courage. But you look down one more time into the perfect, uncompromised white water of sacred purity where your own dark burden disappeared forever, then back to these anxious faces again, and your steps toward them grow stronger and braver as you move to complete the relief you've already begun on that perfect gold-flecked sparkling bridge God built just for you.

Now, armed with that strength and courage and the momentum from this medita-

tion, bring yourself back, open your eyes, feeling lighter already from the burden of guilt you left behind, and make real the rightness you began with each one of those people you saw waiting, sad and afraid, in the green meadow.

THE AFFIRMATION

"I am part of God, just as He is part of me. Today I will honor Him by learning from guilt without embracing it or perpetuating it. I will lighten my burden by taking action to resolve what guilt I've earned, and what unearned guilt I'm carrying I now release forever into the white light of the Holy Spirit."

8

Children

However you feel about Hillary Clinton, please don't let politics influence your opinion of a saying she popularized: It really *does* take a village to raise a child. More "primitive" cultures have known and practiced that fact for centuries. It's the ego of our "civilized" culture that's caused a minority of people to try to argue with it, with such shortsighted remarks as "It takes a good, solid, healthy *family* to raise a child, that's what it takes." I guess those people are living in some cave where the divorce rate isn't well over fifty percent, unwanted pregnancy is unheard of, all biological parents are responsible people, and every family is good, solid, and healthy. I have no idea where that cave is, but you'd think it would be more widely publicized if it existed, wouldn't you? For the rest of us, living in reality, there is no such thing as a child whose welfare is none of our concern.

Thank God that fact is becoming more and more obvious, and laws and organizations to protect, defend, and rescue children throughout the world are growing stronger by the day. While we still have a long way to go, there's a glimmer of optimism to be found in our increasing insistence that neglect, abuse, disrespect, or disregard toward *any* child is unacceptable and a crime against all of us who have even a shred of compassion and morality.

Politics and the divorce rate aside, why does the centuries-old observation that it takes a village to raise a child strike such a strong chord of truth today?

It's not just because we know that the government's system of helping our children is flawed, understaffed, underfunded, and overloaded.

It's not just because we know that the Internet is providing a whole new twisted, horrible playground for pedophiles to cruise.

It's not just because violence against and among children is more openly publicized and more impossible to ignore than ever before.

It's not just because of the indisputable fact that children are our future and our greatest natural human resource.

It's also because, as spirituality continues to spread and flourish, so does the realization, whether we're consciously aware of it or not, that children are our closest human link to our own immortality on The Other Side.

Where Children Come From

No, don't brace yourself for a tedious biology lesson. I assume you already know how babies' physical bodies are created. If you don't, ask around. You won't believe it.

Babies' spirits, on the other hand, arrive directly from full, busy lives at Home, after a very difficult, deliberate decision to return here to advance their progress on the eternal path toward their greatest potential. Inside those tiny, fragile, preverbal bodies live souls as ageless and timeless as ours, with memories of past lives and of The Other

Side that are fresh, clear, and unedited. And those memories linger in their conscious minds for years before the business of life on earth overwhelms them. It's no different than our returning from an extended visit to a place we deeply love—for quite a while, our bodies may be back from the trip, but our heads and hearts are still preoccupied with that other wonderful place.

Because they're so much closer to The Other Side and their past lives than we are, children are the most psychic humans on earth, and we can learn as much from them as we'll allow about Home, the spirit world, reincarnation, astral travel, and all the other marvelous bridges between here and eternity. What's sadly fascinating is, we have endless evidence that children are already very sophisticated beings when they arrive, and yet we carelessly ignore that evidence, mislabel it, make silly excuses for it, and/or fail to explore it.

If you've spent any time with young children, you know that they have interests, gifts, fears, phobias, and preferences that make all the sense in the world when you take past lives into account and no sense at all when you don't. Children are born mesmerized by trains, or pirates, or aviation, or tall ships, or the California gold rush, or astronomy, or countless other things to which they couldn't possibly have been exposed in this life. They're born with athletic or musical talent, or a natural affinity for carpentry, or electronics, or architecture, or fashion design, or countless other skills nonexistent in the rest of their family. They're born frightened of dark water, or heights, or bridges, or being alone, or crowds of people, or small places, or countless other places or circumstances they've never confronted this time around, phobias not necessarily shared by anyone else they spend time with.

The lame explanation that all those unique qualities are thanks to some combination of genetics and environment falls apart pretty quickly when you can't find a likely source for those qualities in anyone or anything around that child. There's also an old wives' tale that all these interests, phobias, and preferences can be traced to the mother's reading and viewing habits during her pregnancy. Wouldn't you love to know what Mozart's mother read while she was pregnant that produced a child who could compose operas by the time he was five years old? And then there's my personal favorite, the shrug accompanied by an almost authoritative "It just happens," which is invariably a cover for the more truthful "I don't have the slightest idea." Do any of those explanations even come close to making as much sense as the simple fact of retained memories from past lives? Reincarnation has been scoffed at so often as some sort of far-out, goofy, woo-woo myth. Children are the best argument of all that, in fact, reincarnation is just plain old commonsense logic.

I've given countless examples in other books of young children's ability to recount stories from previous lifetimes and experiences on The Other Side. Not the least of these is my son Chris who, when he was three years old, told me about being a cowboy in a past life, with a horse named Cinnamon, and dying of a gunshot wound in the street in front of a saloon while his daughter held his head. As with all children recalling other incarnations, the details of a story like this were far beyond the typical vocabulary and imagination of a child his age. And my granddaughter, Angelia, has active, precise memories of her last life as my treasured Grandma Ada. But please don't try to dismiss those instances as being unique to my family because of our long psychic legacy. They're common, they're exciting to discover, and they can work wonders on the communication between you and your children, and on their self-confidence when they sense your interest, your eagerness to listen without dismissing them, and their reality being acknowledged as important.

A perfect case in point was a couple who came to me recently with their six-year-old son, hoping I could get to the bottom of his obsessive interest in anything and everything to do with the *Titanic* disaster. The obsession had existed in him as far back as they could remember, and certainly started long before the recent megamovie came out, a tape of which he had watched countless times, often pointing out what he swore were inaccuracies in the film. They wanted me to find out what was "wrong" with him, their biggest fear seeming to be the unlikely possibility that he had been possessed by the spirit of a *Titanic* passenger. As it turned out, he wasn't possessed at all. His last life actually ended on the *Titanic*, and I didn't need to hypnotically regress him to get that information—spotty as it was in places, he had conscious memories of frigid water, screams drowning out the faint impossible sound of orchestra music, his hand too cold and wet to maintain its hold on the arm of a would-be rescuer in an overcrowded life raft, his last prayer as the roiling ocean pulled him under that his wife had been saved. His parents were almost as amazed at my power as they were at the story inside their son when I told them about it afterward. But the most amazing thing was that all I had done to get their son to tell me his *Titanic* story was the one thing that somehow hadn't occurred to them—I just asked him, and then listened to his answers. They had been so busy trying to analyze him—wondering whether or not his passionate interest in this historic tragedy was healthy, avoiding conversations about it with him out of their own discomfort, and generally worrying about him to the point of distraction—that they never thought of simply sitting down with him and saying, "Tell us what you know about the *Titanic*, sweetheart." If they had done that, and then just calmly heard him out, they would have found him as anxious to talk about it as I did.

From the time your children are able to verbalize their thoughts, ask them questions, in an encouraging tone, about anything they express special interest in, or even about previous lives or The Other Side in general, such as "Who were you before this?" or "How many other mothers have you had?" or "Tell me about the place you were before you came here." Don't force or suggest answers, just let them talk or not talk, at their own pace, so that they know you're receptive to the conversation whenever they're ready. Never judge the answers you get, but do yourself and them a favor—record the answers, in a journal or on tape, so that years later, when their memories have inevitably dimmed, they'll have comforting proof that there was a time when they knew all about their own immortality.

Children and Cell Memory

The "Past Lives" chapter discusses cell memory at some length—the emotional and physiological impact the spirit's memories of past lives can have on us in our current life, as our spirit reacts to the familiar experience of being in a body again. And even preverbal children, with such fresh past-life memories and such open and guileless minds, are very susceptible to the negative affects of cell memory and very easy to "cure" as well.

I've dealt with hundreds and hundreds of children suffering from cell-memory problems, most of them referrals from doctors who had had no success with traditional treatments. (Let me repeat, I will always urge everyone to seek traditional medical and psychiatric help *first* when an illness presents itself, especially with children. My own grandchildren have ongoing relationships with wonderful doctors and psychologists, so please don't ever misread anything I say as a claim that we legitimate psychics are substitutes for those professionals, or that we're instant cure-alls for every physical or emotional problem.) Just one example was a four-year-old girl named Chelsea, who was born with severe asthma that didn't respond to any medications her doctors had tried. What conscious memories she had of past lives didn't reveal any answers, so I did a hypnotic regression on her—a breeze with young children, by the way. And she very quickly got to the root of her asthma: In the incarnation immediately before this one, she had been a rancher named Jack Shepherd, who'd been wrongly accused of stealing a neighbor's horse and hanged for the crime. It was a slow, horrible death, with Shepherd desperately and unsuccessfully struggling to breathe—a cell memory that poor Chelsea's spirit had retained and brought with it into this tiny little girl's body in the form of an illness that literally took her breath away.

I was able to help Chelsea the way I've helped hundreds of other children, whether or not they were even old enough to talk, by speaking to the wise, mature spirit mind in the child's subconscious, during either hypnosis or sleep. You can easily help a child close to you in exactly the same way, before or after cell-memory problems have started showing up. And it really is this simple:

Once or twice a week, while the child sleeps, sit down quietly beside them and, in a low voice that won't wake them, tell their spirit mind, "Precious child, may all the joy, wisdom, and lessons of your past lives be your constant companions to help you through this life. But let all the pain, fear, illness, and negativity from those lives fall away into the past where they belong and then be released forever into the healing purity of the Holy Spirit's sacred white light."

In case you're skeptical that this easy exercise can make a genuine difference in your child's physical and emotional health, let me assure you, so were most of the clients I've recommended it to, who wrote months later to tell me it worked. And if that doesn't convince you, look at it this way—on the off chance that I'm right, what possible harm can it do to try?

Children and the Spirit World

Because they're still so fresh from the higher vibrational frequency of The Other Side, and because they haven't yet been told that there's anything inappropriate or odd about it, the vast majority of children interact with spirits and ghosts as if they were "imaginary friends." You'll be missing a fascinating experience if you dismiss these "imaginary" friends with a patronizing "That's nice, dear," instead of asking questions and finding out everything you can about them. Beyond the name of the imaginary friend, where did they come from? What do they look like? How did your child meet them? Have they known each other before? If so, where did they know each other? What do the two of them talk about?

My son Chris had two imaginary friends, and we talked about them as freely and openly as we talked about his "real" friends. One turned out to be his Spirit Guide, Charley, whom Chris has never since been able to see as clearly as he could when he was a child. The other was a little boy named Joey, who gave me an opportunity to teach Chris a wonderful lesson in unselfish love when he was still very young. One day Chris mentioned, almost in passing, that Joey was, as he put it, "all burned." If your child ever describes their imaginary friend as having an injury, it's a red flag—that friend is an earthbound, or ghost. Once we make a full transition to The Other Side, we're whole and perfect, and injuries simply don't exist. Only earthbound spirits will have visible injuries. Having a ghost around your child doesn't mean your child is in danger. It means that the spirit doesn't know it's dead and is either refusing the legendary light of the tunnel Home or staying behind out of some confused attachment to this dimension where it no longer belongs. When I explained to Chris that we needed to help Joey go to The Other Side, his first reaction was that he didn't want his friend to leave. But once he understood that Joey couldn't be happy here with so few people able to see and hear him, and that when he was at Home with God and all the people who loved him he'd be happy and not "all burned" anymore, he willingly said good-bye and we talked Joey to the light toward The Other Side together.

Once you get a few clues to the identity of your child's imaginary friend, you can enhance the experience even more by checking out property records, photographs, and family histories. I can't begin to guess how many children I've worked with who were able to point out their imaginary friend in snapshots of decades-old family or neighborhood gatherings, or how many of their imaginary friends' names turned up on an obscure branch of the family tree from several generations ago, or on lists of previous owners of the land on which the house now sits.

In other words, just *pay attention.* Humoring your child about their imaginary friend without encouraging them to talk about it could deprive you of a direct line to the spirit world, while depriving your child of the invaluable feeling of being taken seriously.

Also, one of the most consistent facts of the spirit world is that spirits leap at every opportunity to be seen and heard, and children, with their heightened, unedited psychic senses, provide some of their best opportunities. Take it from someone who's slept with a light on since I was a child, spirits will happily gather in the darkness of a receptive person's bedroom at night. From the time I was just learning to walk, I felt as if I were trying to sleep in the middle of Grand Central Station when I was alone in my room with the bedside lamp turned off. It's not that these spirits had any desire to hurt me or frighten me, they were just enthusiastic and eager for attention. Was I afraid? Are you kidding? You bet I was, until my dear Grandma Ada patiently explained who all these strangers gathering around my bed every night were, without anyone else in the family seeming to mind or even notice. Once I understood what was going on, and that I was in no danger, I was much less afraid than just annoyed—I do love an audience, but not while I'm trying to sleep, thanks.

So if and when your child wakes up frightened during the night and tells you there was someone or something in their room, first search the room, the closet, and under the bed, just to make sure the *really* scary possibility—a human being—is ruled out. Then, instead of the tired old explanation "You're imagining things," which you're very probably wrong about anyway, assure your child that they're safe and that their visitor or visitors were undoubtedly spirits from The Other Side, wanting to say hello and watch over them. Again, have your child describe what they saw, and don't hesitate to record these sightings, too, in a journal or on tape, to see if there are any "regulars" in the group and for fascinating reading for you and your child a decade or two down the line. Finally, at least get them a night-light, or do what Grandma Ada did for me and provide them with a flashlight to keep beside their bed. Whether it's frightening or just irritating, a dark room filling with spirits is not conducive to a good night's sleep, for you and especially for your child.

A Child's Dreams

Some children's dreams are just like some of ours, nothing more than little vaudeville shows our subconscious minds put on for meaningless comic relief. But others are full of valuable information and very much worth paying attention to.

Astral travel comes naturally to most children, for the logical reason that it's what they've been accustomed to at Home, where we get where we want to go by simply thinking ourselves there. The easiest time for astral travel is during sleep, when the conscious mind won't interfere, and children's favorite destination when they astrally travel is the familiar, blessed sanctity of The Other Side.

If your child tells you about a "dream" that's even slightly in sequence, with a beginning, middle, and end, as opposed to scattered images that don't make much sense, chances are it wasn't a dream at all but an astral trip instead. Pay particular attention to stories about playing with other children on a vast stone stairway in front of a gleaming white stone building, and about walking in a beautiful lush garden, often with a grown-up with whom the child felt safe and loved. As I described in my book *Life on The Other Side,* the steps leading to the Hall of Wisdom and the magnificent gardens of the Hall of Justice are visited several times a week by the spirits of children who have incarnated, and the gardens are trea- sured spots for children's spirits to hold re- unions with friends and loved ones at Home. The crowds of children playing on the steps of the Hall of Wisdom have been known to be so rowdy, in fact, that my Spirit Guide, Francine, once asked me to speak to my son Chris about his being a little too playful during his frequent visits to those steps and disrupting the constant stream of spirits coming and going from that sacred Hall.

Children don't limit their astral travel dur- ing sleep to trips to The Other Side. They also enjoy checking in on friends and rela- tives, and people and places they've known in past lives. Again, listen for "dreams" that have a sequential order, especially if they involved flying. Flying almost always indicates an astral trip instead of a dream, and if the child remembers any details at all, ask them what they could look down and see while they were flying. If the landscape they describe is a place they couldn't possibly be familiar with in this lifetime, there's a very good chance they took advantage of the opportunity sleep provided to reminisce about some previous incarnation they've never forgotten.

I'm sorry to keep repeating myself (actually, I don't mind a bit), but please keep a written or taped record of your child's "dreams." You'll learn so much about your child, and about their easy access to The Other Side and past lives and the spirit world that you experienced at their age but sadly don't remember, and they'll cherish proof of those "dreams" long after their memories of them have faded.

A Few Added Tips for and about Children

- **Never underestimate how psychic and ageless children really are.** I literally shudder when I hear people discuss anger, violence, abuse, tension, or neglect in a home where a child is living and claim, "They're too young to know what's going on." That's not just untrue, it's impossible. I don't care if a child is a year old, a week old, or an hour old. They have an uncanny awareness of what's going on every minute, and a spirit that, like ours, has been around for an eternity, as capable as ours of feeling frightened, unsafe, unwanted, and demeaned, especially in such a tiny, defenseless body.

- **Be as respectful to children as you are to your best friend.** I've never understood why some people seem to believe there's a minimum age for treating a human being with common courtesy. A two-year-old can appreciate *please, thank you,* and *excuse me* every bit as much as a twenty-two-year-old, and it's insane to scold a child for rudeness when it's the exact behavior they're on the receiving end of on a daily basis. Whether it's grabbing the TV remote without asking and switching channels from a show your child is watching, or stepping past or in front of a stranger's child in a store as if there's no one standing there, we all have to watch carefully for ways in which we might be contributing to making any child feel unimportant.

- **Never let *any* other relationship become a higher priority than your relationship with your child.** That statement seems so obvious, but we've all known someone who's found it easy to ignore, and it's a tragic mistake that will take several lifetimes to correct. No chart is written on The Other Side that allows for a parent to sacrifice the safety, security, and welfare of their own child for the sake of anything or anyone that comes along. The temptations themselves are charted, but they're there to resist on the child's behalf, not to indulge in with a stream of self-justifying excuses.

- **If you can't name three productive things your child is good at, you're not looking hard enough.** Every one of us chooses gifts and shortcomings to work with throughout each lifetime, and children are no exception. Helping a child find skills they're good at won't just help their self-confidence, it will significantly lower the chances of their being bored and hitting the streets for stimulation when they're older. I don't care if it's a sport, mechanical work, gardening, computers, art, a musical instrument, gymnastics, hairdressing, sewing, writing, carpentry—even very young children display talents, preferences, and interests that you can encourage and guide them to pursue. Just make sure they're your child's interests, not yours. You've got your chart, your children have theirs.

- **From the moment your child is born, teach them about their sacred connection, and every living thing's connection, to God.** I'm not necessarily talking about making sure children attend church regularly, or learn religious dogma by rote. I know people, and I'm sure you do, too, who never miss a Sunday service and maybe even can recite the Bible from beginning to end, and yet they're cruel, selfish, judgmental, bigoted, and utterly joyless. The more aware children are of their God-center, and the God-center of all of His creations, the more respect they'll demand and give throughout their lives.

- **Next time you're sitting around thinking you have nothing to do, take a moment to realize that at the same time, there's a child who could use your help.** Whether it's a nearby pediatric hospital, a charity for needy children, an organization to help locate missing children, or a school or library where children are being read to or are learning to read, there's a place not far from you where you can make a difference in just one child's life, and that's not just a pleasure, it's a privilege you and the journey of your spirit will cherish quite literally for an eternity.

THE AFFIRMATION

"Dear Father and Mother God,

"Please help us protect our children, just as you protect all of us who are Your children. Teach us to keep them safe from bodily and emotional harm, and to celebrate the joy and dignity of knowing that with every step they take in this hard, rough school of earth, Your Hand will never leave theirs and Your Light will let them see the path ahead more clearly, no matter how much it winds through the inevitable threatening darkness. We are blessed by the very presence of Your smallest and youngest arrivals among us, and it is our oath to You to care for them as surely as if they were all our own. Amen."

9

Relationships

His name was Jack, and he'd flown twelve hundred miles in a chartered plane for his reading. He was a very handsome man in his late forties and wore his Armani suit and gold Rolex as comfortably as most of us wear our favorite sweats. Two things struck me the moment he walked into my office: There was an older, elegant female spirit right behind him, and for a man with such obvious advantages, he looked awfully unhappy.

The female spirit was gesturing and chirping at me, eager to communicate, and I thought she might be part of the cause of his unhappiness, so before Jack had even settled into his chair, I said, "Who's the tall, slender, sophisticated older woman who's passed—heart-shaped face, high cheekbones, piercing hazel eyes, grayish-white upswept hair, and beautiful hands?"

"That's my mother," he replied, his voice oddly flat. "She died four months ago. We were very close."

"She's with you right now, standing beside you, touching your shoulder."

I expected surprise, relief, a smile, or at the very least a glimmer of curiosity. What I got was "Okay, but you've got to tell me about my fiancée. I think she's cheating on me."

Variations on that scene play themselves out in my office a dozen times a week, reinforcing one simple, indisputable fact: Our relationships with the people we choose as lovers and spouses can consume us more completely, for better or worse, than almost any other facet of life. They can make our spirit soar or make it crumble. They can expand our heart or make us wish we didn't have one. They can inspire our greatest sense of freedom or hold us hostage, and make everything we've ever accomplished feel important or utterly worthless. Take

Jack, for example, who would have traded all his privileges for the fidelity he wasn't getting from his fiancée; who believed in me enough to charter a plane for a reading but, when I confirmed his fear that he was being cheated on, argued with me, went home, and spent thousands of dollars for a private detective who proved that I was right; who, despite his undeniable intelligence, married his fiancée when her lover dumped her and then spent three miserable years with a chronically unfaithful woman he knew from the beginning he couldn't trust.

Believe me, I'm not making fun of Jack, nor am I throwing stones. I've made my share of idiotic choices in my life when it comes to relationships, and since about ninety percent of my clients and close friends have, too, I've spent a lot of time trying to figure out where and how the vast majority of us seem to go wrong.

Relationships and Our Chart

There's no question that we include all our relationships in our chart. And because we're very specific when we write our chart, it's not surprising that when we meet someone with whom we've preplanned a relationship, we recognize them, sometimes immediately. If you've ever wondered where the concept of "love at first sight" comes from, now you know. It's not really love at first sight, but it is "I wrote you into my chart, and there you are!" at first sight. Instant recognition, or even recognition that takes its time washing over us, feels amazingly significant. Unfortunately, we misread that significance far too often, and that's where a lot of our troubles begin—it rarely occurs to us that this person we're so overwhelmed at recognizing just might be one of those people we charted to avoid like the plague. When I say we chart all our relationships, I do mean *all,* both the good ones and the disastrous ones.

We've all known people who cling fiercely to someone who mistreats them, demeans them, and keeps them in a constant state of insecure misery. Just as we sometimes make the mistake of believing God didn't answer our prayer when in fact He did answer, He just said no, we have trouble remembering that some of the most important relationships we chart, from which our spirits profit the most, are those to which *we* have the strength to say no.

So how do we know the difference between charted relationships we're supposed to pursue and ones we're supposed to avoid?

The answers to that question aren't easy, and they take work, patience, and a lot of self-honesty. But considering the joy those answers can bring you and the pain they can spare you, they're worth all the work, patience, and self-honesty you can give them and more, don't you think?

1. Be Patient

This isn't an opinion, it's a fact: Most people are more careful about choosing a car than they are about choosing a Significant Other.

Since you can "afford" any quality of relationship you demand, let's say you go off to shop for a car with enough money to buy any vehicle on the market. Now, imagine your selection process going like this: "I really had my heart set on a Rolls-Royce, but then I saw this used red Pinto with a For Sale sign on it, and I've always liked red. I wanted a four-door, and this Pinto is only a two-door, and I was hoping for something six people can sit in comfortably, but four people can squeeze into this Pinto if they try hard enough. I love listening to music while I drive, but the Pinto has no radio or speakers. It's very important to me to have reliable transportation to get back and forth to work, and apparently this Pinto only starts every once in a while and will suddenly die on the road for no reason. Naturally, I was hoping for something safe, and I've heard this car has a history of exploding every once in a while, but that's okay—*it's better than having no car at all, and I'm sure if I drive it long enough, it will turn into a Rolls-Royce."*

As idiotic as that sounds, haven't you seen (or been through) that same approach toward the decision about whether or not to enter into a relationship? We go out in search of a Rolls-Royce and come home with a broken-down Pinto only because it was on the market and it was red, and we're surprised when we find ourselves disappointed later? Is it *really* better than no car at all, or have we just let ourselves be convinced that we're nobody if we don't have a car? And do we *really* think a broken-down, unreliable Pinto that might explode at any moment is the best we deserve, or, if there are children involved, the best they deserve?

I promise you, as soon as we start truly appreciating ourselves for the children of God that we are, we'll start demanding the quality of life and relationships a child of God deserves and never settle for less than that. We all chart plenty of Pintos for ourselves along the way, not to accept them but to learn to finally say, "Not good enough!" and hold out for those rare Rolls-Royces we also charted if we'll just be patient and have enough faith to insist on nothing but the finest there is.

Once we've promised ourself that we're not interested in anything but the best, it's time to start defining what our idea of "the best" really is. And a variation on making a list of how we define "the best" can help a lot.

2. Make a List

At some time or other, either mentally or on paper, we've all made a list of the qualities we are looking for in a mate. The list usually contains items like "attractive, responsible, good natured, considerate, trustworthy, reliable, kind, and likes children." And then we'll go right on saying yes to people who have few if any of those qualities as if we never made that list in the first place, which is what made me start wondering if there might be a more worthwhile list to make, one that could bring us a little more clarity.

Instead of listing the qualities of your ideal mate, I want you to list the qualities of the mate you've got now, or the last mate you had for some length of time, but precede each item on your list with the words *What I want most is a mate who . . . ,* and this is a good time to remind you again, *be honest.* A typical list might look like this:

- *What I want most is a mate who* criticizes everything I do.
- *What I want most is a mate who* is likely to cheat on me at the slightest opportunity.
- *What I want most is a mate who* routinely lies to me.
- *What I want most is a mate who* disrespects me, calls me insulting names, and never compliments me.
- *What I want most is a mate who* tries to control my every move.

- *What I want most is a mate who* is verbally, emotionally, or physically abusive.
- *What I want most is a mate who* is unkind to my/our children.
- *What I want most is a mate who* is rude to my family and friends.
- *What I want most is a mate who* is unreliable and irresponsible.
- *What I want most is a mate who* enjoys embarrassing me.
- *What I want most is a mate who* spends our bill money on gambling, drugs, or alcohol abuse.

Obviously that list might be a little extreme, but I'm sure you get the point: If your list seems rational when you reread it, you're in a relationship you charted yourself to pursue. If it seems ludicrous and completely illogical, you're wasting time in a relationship you charted to gain strength from by walking away, no matter how hard it might be.

3. Live Your Chart, Not the Myth

We all know the myth: We're supposed to grow up, get our education, date through our high school and possibly college years to get some experience with relationships, fall in love, get married, probably have children, balance marriage and children with careers, probably have and spoil our grandchildren, and then retire happily into the sunset with the same spouse we started with.

I'm not about to claim that that never happens, and it's a gorgeous thing to see when it does. I just wish we would start thinking of it as a relatively rare option, as opposed to an expectation and/or the only way we'll find happiness and be successful. There are more than six billion people on earth, which means there are more than six billion charts being lived out right now. Does it really make sense to believe that the vast majority of six billion people, each with our own lessons to learn and purposes for being here, planned to accomplish such an infinite variety of goals through "get married, have children, have grandchildren, go Home"?

I promise you, we'd see a drop in the divorce rate if we could let go of the idea that there's something wrong with us if we aren't married by a certain age, or if we never get married at all. We've all known people who got married to someone they didn't even particularly enjoy, let alone love, because "it was time," or "we'd been together for so long, it seemed like the logical thing to do," or "there was a baby on the way, and a child deserves two parents." You know what else a child deserves? A home with love at its core, not resentment and obligation and tension, and many children can get that much more effectively if the two parents stay close and civil and actively involved in the children's lives without forcing a relationship that one or both of the parents don't really want.

I lost track decades ago of the number of clients who've asked, "When will I get married?" Not "When will I have a good, solid, healthy relationship?" Some of that is attributable to knowing they wrote marriage into their charts and getting anxious about it. But more of it is attributable to confused priorities, based more on the myth than the chart. I'm also fascinated by the number of clients who are letting the myth rather than the chart dictate their idea of how the timing and progress of their relationship should go. "Steve and I have been very happy and committed to each other for two years," a client named Lorraine once told me. "I think it's about time we move in together, but he's dragging his feet about it." She owned a house she loved. So did he. They both had jobs in which they did a lot of their work at home. They both appreciated their privacy. She had three dogs. He had a dog and two cats. I pointed out that combining households could easily end up making them and their animals miserable. She replied, "I know, that's what he says, but after two years, it seems like if he loves me he should want to live with me." In other words, "Of course we'd be miserable, but I've picked two years as the arbitrary time frame in which I think we're supposed to take this step that doesn't make any sense for either one of us, so that he can prove something I already know." To top things off, I told Lorraine that she had a choice: She and Steve could continue their wonderful relationship for another twelve years if they left their living arrangement as it was, or she could convince him to move in, and they'd be together another eight months at most. And she had trouble deciding which she'd prefer. Lorraine was as good an example as I've seen of letting the myth override the chart, and sure enough, she chose the myth and she and Steve broke up seven and a half months later.

So as best you can—remembering that none of us are quite in our right minds when we're in love—when you're trying to determine if your relationship is one that you charted to pursue or to avoid, take a long, hard, honest look at whether your interest in it is in *any* way connected more to the myth than to your own unique chart, designed to guide you toward a joy only you can truly define.

4. Respect

At the heart of every successful relationship lies *respect.* Or, to put it another way, at the heart of every doomed relationship lies *disrespect.* If you're in a relationship in which you either don't respect your partner or aren't respected by your partner, I guarantee this is a relationship you charted for yourself to learn from and leave, it's that simple. And the sooner the better, too, since I'm a big believer that the longer you postpone the inevitable, the more time in this life you waste.

In case you're wondering about love and trust and all those other important ingredients of a good relationship, the more you think about it the more you'll realize that without respect, they either don't mean much or they can't exist at all. The great thing about respect is that when it exists, in its deepest and most honest form, it eliminates a lot of the destructive behavior that can tear apart a relationship and the people in it. When you truly respect someone, you don't lie to them, or cheat on them, or demean them, or steal from them, or speak badly about them, or try to control them, or invade their privacy, or ignore what's important to them, or want anything more for them than their highest potential and their most glorious dreams.

If you happen to be in a relationship in which you're being chronically disrespected, I want to warn you about a trap many of my clients in that situation fall into far too easily. They believe that if they hang in their long enough, putting up with any and all disrespect their partner dishes out, it will somehow prove to their partner how much they love them, and then someday, the depth of their love finally realized, they'll *earn* the respect they've been yearning for. The comment to me is usually some version of "After all they've put me through, sooner or later they're bound to figure out that no one else will ever love them as much as I do." Sadly, that's just plain not true, for a simple, logical reason I hope you'll memorize if any of this sounds too familiar: *You never earn respect by tolerating disrespect.* Not ever. In fact, one of the questions the client's partner frequently asks is "If I treat you so badly, why don't you leave?" And unfortunately, the typical answer is "Because I love you," which only gives the message "I'll love you no matter how much you disrespect me, so you can keep right on doing it all you want, there won't be any consequences." Hard as it is, there's only one thing you can do to earn respect from a partner who's in the habit of disrespecting you. You have to distance yourself from them, not just emotionally but physically. Don't threaten to leave unless you mean it, and when you mean it, do it. If you can't do it for yourself and your God-center that deserves respect and is charted to demand it, do it for your partner, and the lesson they need to learn that for every act of disrespect, there really is a price to pay.

Addiction

At first glance, addiction might seem like a topic that doesn't belong in a chapter about relationships. But if you're in a relationship that involves abuse—verbal, emotional, or physical—and can't bring yourself to leave because you think you love the person who's abusing you, you need to consider the distinct probability that you're not in love, you're in the grip of a serious addiction and need every bit of as much urgent, radical, possibly lifesaving help as any other addict.

In some ways, addiction to an abusive person or situation is even tougher to break than addiction to a substance. For one thing, the medical, scientific, and psychiatric communities have been hard at work for decades on active ways to conquer substance abuse—at the very least it's easier to identify and trace the body's chemical responses to alcohol and various drugs so that antidotes can be developed. Doctors are having increasing success with a treatment in which addicts are essentially put to sleep for forty-eight hours and, with the help of IVs and monitors, put through withdrawal and detoxified, with a time-release implant added so that the substance in question will have no effect in the future. Twelve-step programs, support groups, and in-patient clinics are everywhere, available twenty-four hours a day throughout the world, and substance addiction is finally being recognized as the very genuine critical illness that it is. But there's no IV, antidote, or detox program that can even begin to help the body and mind do battle against addiction to another person and eliminate the psychological need for that person that the addict is up against. It would be a great contribution to society if the medical, scientific, and psychiatric communities would pool their resources as they have in the war against substance abuse and declare war on this equally devastating human addiction as well.

For another thing, while there's no rational way to romanticize substance abuse, someone who's addicted to an abusive person can come up with countless ways to romanticize their determination to hang in there and refuse to leave. Strong addiction, after all, can feel like profound love. Need and dependence can feel like passion. Relationships in general are more encouraged than discouraged, which gives the addict a false sense of being involved in something that's thought of as socially "normal." If there are children involved, the addict can claim they're staying for their children's sake, with the hollow every-child-deserves-two-parents excuse. And if the addict was raised around abuse and has come to equate abuse with love, the addiction might be actively pursued without the addict even understanding that that's what they're doing and believe it's somehow "just their luck" to attract abusers.

For yet another thing, breaking a substance addiction obviously requires that the addict completely eliminate that substance from their lives, for the rest of their lives. But when the object of the addiction is an abusive person, that abusive person might not have any interest in letting go of all this power and control and will make every effort to pursue and win back the addict. Accessible as it is, alcohol isn't likely to pick up the phone and call ten or fifteen times a day. Seductive as cocaine can be, it won't show up at the door with flowers and a lovely forgive-me note. Marijuana can't play the let's-stay-together-for-the-sake-of-the-children card, and heroin doesn't apologize, behave itself for a few days or weeks, and promise never to let the abuse happen again. So until and unless the abuser is willing to leave the addict completely alone and refuse any communication from the addict, overcoming this particular addiction can be the toughest fight the addict will ever face, *and the most gratifying, worthwhile fight to win.*

I've learned from countless clients, from the medical and psychiatric doctors I work with all over the country, and from having survived and walked away from an abusive marriage myself that there are ways to tell if you've actually become addicted to a relationship. Here are just a few of the guaranteed tip-offs:

- If your only justification for staying in an emotionally, mentally, or physically abusive relationship is "because I love him/her," *you're not in love, you're addicted.*
- If the best interests of your partner or the relationship come first, above and be-

yond the best interests of your children, *you're not in love, you're addicted.*

- If you cover up and lie for your partner's behavior and/ or any injuries you've suffered, *you're not in love, you're addicted.*
- If family and friends who love you and have always given you rock-solid advice and support are all begging you to get out, and you've decided that somehow, suddenly, out of nowhere, for no reason, all those same people are ganging up on you, or are jealous, or too judgmental, or too involved in something that's none of their business, *you're not in love, you're addicted.*
- If you know in your heart that the *healthy* thing to do is leave, but you stay anyway, *you're not in love, you're addicted.*
- If you've read this section several times with a sinking feeling in your soul and are promising yourself that you're going to do something about it "if things don't get better," *you're not in love, you're addicted.*

And if it turns out that, yes, you are addicted, *please* accept the fact that, just like any victim of substance abuse, you have a potentially fatal illness and you need every bit as much urgent professional care as any other addict. Don't waste one more moment feeling ashamed. The only shame is in not doing something about it once you've recognized it.

Sooner or later, the medical, scientific, and psychiatric communities will start focusing major efforts on this particularly insidious form of addiction. But until then, thank God, there are some wonderful organizations who are ready, willing, and able to help you twenty-four hours a day, seven days a week, if you'll only speak up and ask. Write down the following phone numbers, and if you can't bring yourself to dial one of them right now, keep them with you at all times so that you'll be ready to call when the right moment comes: (800) 799-SAFE; (800) ENDABUSE; and (800) 978-3600. Or, if it would make you feel more comfortable and make the help feel less anonymous, call my office at (408) 379-7070 and/or e-mail us at www.sylvia.org and let my staff, my ministers, and me guide you toward the path to your joyful recovery and the life as a victorious survivor that your chart promised and your God-center demands.

In Search of Ms. or Mr. Right

Notice that I didn't say "in search of your soul mate." I'm not even going to go into this at length, because I've carried on about it in depth on television and in my previous books *The Other Side and Back* and *Life on The Other Side.* But the short version is, *don't knock yourself out trying to find your soul mate!* Your soul mate is your twin soul, created at the same moment you were, spiritually identical, with perfect compatibility. It is not the other half of you, because you are not half a person. Your soul mate isn't necessarily someone you'll be romantically connected to. In fact, it's likely that they're not even passing through, this time around, as your romantic gender of preference, or your romantic age of preference, or, most importantly, they're probably not even passing through this particular lifetime at the same brief period you are. I can almost promise you that while you're getting depressed searching every nook, cranny, Internet chat room, and singles club for your soul mate, your soul mate is having a great time on The Other Side planning your "welcome Home" party. So stop setting yourself up for one disappointment after another, give up this soul-mate fixation, and appreciate the *kindred souls,* or compatible and familiar spirits, you've charted for yourself along the way in this life.

There. That having been said, I only have one reliable tip to my clients for finding the healthy relationships they're looking for, and I offer the same to you, warning you up front that it might not be what you want to hear. But it's this simple and this seemingly contradictory: *The sure way to find a healthy relationship is to learn to love your independence and the pleasure of your own company.*

There's nothing more attractive to an emotionally healthy person than someone who's strong, happy, secure, and self-sufficient enough to be selective about their relationships, and who pursues relationships out of genuine interest instead of neediness, based on the certainty that they themselves have a lot to offer. I wouldn't even have to be psychic to spot the difference instantly between clients who want to find Ms. or Mr. Right out of a self-assured desire to build on an already good life and those who are on a quietly desperate search for someone to *give* them a life. As you've seen yourself many times in

many other situations, you can sense someone who lives from a position of strength,
just as surely as you can sense someone
whose very essence is shadowed by the fear
and desperation of believing that by themselves they're incomplete.

If you haven't learned yet how to be your
own best friend and thoroughly enjoy your
own company, I would love for you to pause
right now and either read or reread the "Joy"
chapter in this book, and make a deal with
yourself that you'll devote just ten short minutes a day for one month to any of the exercises in that chapter that appeals to you
most. It's not an accident that none of those
exercises are designed for anyone but *you,*
to help keep you connected to your sacred
God-center, because the more you recognize your own exquisite value, the more you'll
prefer being alone to settling for anything
less than everything a treasured child of God
deserves.

To the Rest of You

As I said earlier in this chapter, there really is such a thing as a healthy, solid,
happy, committed relationship, and I don't

want those of you who are in one to feel left out of this discussion. In fact, congratulations, good for you for being so clearly in synch with that aspect of your chart, and don't you dare let anyone try to convince you that you lucked your way into it. Like everyone else, you're the result of the choices you've made so far, so you're to be admired for choosing to hold out for and demand the best.

Just do yourself and each other one favor that will help you keep up the good work: *Never let a day go by when you don't find some way, no matter how subtle, to say, "Thank God we followed our chart and found each other, not to complete each other, because we were each complete when we met, but to inspire each other to be even finer and more joyful than we would have been alone."*

The Exercise

I want you to sense yourself as a round, hollow, gleaming silver tube, through which the divine gold-white light of God shines with the intense precision of a sacred spotlight into your spirit, cleansing away your fear, your insecurity, your self-doubt, and centering your soul as a perfect balance of intellect and emotion.

As you feel that light creating a healing, joyful heat deep inside you, say to yourself in quiet, whispered truth, "I am part of God, just as He is part of me, and together He and I form a whole, intact, strong, confident, self-sufficient being. I need no other human being in this life to validate my worth, because my worth is my own God-center, bestowed on me by no one else but God, with his divine promise that He will never, ever take it away. All other human beings I invite into my world are in addition to it, a bonus, complementing my already rich, full life but not essential to its existence, just as I can complement their existence without demanding to be essential to it as well."

The gold-white light telescopes even more now, into a fine, glimmering, delicate thread as strong as steel. From the core of your soul that thread branches out and begins winding its way gently and lovingly through you, threading through every vein, every organ, every cell, warming, healing, cleansing, and enlightening as it goes. Your breath deepens, slows, becoming more rhythmic, and with each exhale you release one more fear of being alone, one more false sense of dependence, one more panic that by yourself you're incomplete, one more obsessive, urgent lie that anyone else but you can make you happy and fulfill your life.

Each inhale comes more easily as the gold-white thread now unwinds itself again, leaving its trail of God's sacred touch behind, withdrawing back to the core of your spirit, gathering and intensifying again into that spotlight, that self-passion, that absolute certainty that you and He are all you need, and the rest must earn their way into your heart with the respect, trust, honesty, loyalty, and unconditional love that every blessed child of God deserves.

THE AFFIRMATION

"Dear God,

"I know that with Your guidance I wrote my chart to include many relationships—those to learn from and reject as part of my soul's progress, and those I embrace that help me celebrate my value. I pray for the wisdom and clarity to know the difference, the strength to act on that difference, and the patience to never again settle for anything or anyone whose spiritual growth falls short of mine and blinds them to the God-center I cherish above all else. Amen."

10

Family and Friends

"Fate chooses our relatives, we choose our friends." Did you know that quote was originated by Jacques Delille (1738–1813)? Neither did I. I had to look it up. I wonder if he'd be more of a household name today if he hadn't been wrong.

The truth is, we specifically chose every relative and every friend when we wrote our charts on The Other Side before we came here, based on our needs and goals for this lifetime. If you think I'm turning cartwheels over the fact that we actually have ourselves to thank for those choices, you never met my mother or a couple of in-laws I'd rather not discuss. But I hope it will help you as much as it helps me to remember that we had our reasons for every choice we made. Even the most difficult among them give us opportunities to learn, whether we want to or not, and they're all fascinating in their own ways if we'll open our minds to being fascinated rather than frustrated.

Family History

I'm not talking about the traditional family tree that can help you trace your genetic heritage, significant as that can be. I'm talking about the reality that when we handpick our relatives, we pick some we've never known before who might only be a subplot in this lifetime's story, but we also pick some with whom we share a long, often complicated history of past lives that we're still working our way through.

Even if you don't particularly buy the idea of past lives and past connections, do a scan of everyone in your family just for the fun of it, including aunts, uncles, cousins, in-laws, everyone you're related to, and ask yourself the simple question "Have I known them before?" If you'll keep an open mind and take the first answer that occurs to you,

I'll be surprised if you don't feel an immediate yes or no in response to each person as you focus on them. And the yes or no won't necessarily follow the most logical lines either. You might find yourself feeling no particular connection to a sibling or a parent, while a cousin or great-aunt or nephew could inspire a strong sense that, yes, this is someone you have a history with, for better or worse, that defies the limits of this one lifetime.

My father and I shared many lives together. Both of my sons and I have known each other in several different lives. In fact, one of them, to whom I was married in the twelfth century, kept me locked in a tower where he could keep an eye on me at all times, and nine centuries later he bought me a house on a hilltop directly across from his, far enough away for our respective privacy but still in view enough that he could watch for my lights to go on to make sure I got home safely and on time. One of my daughters-in-law and I shared two past lives, one of my grandsons and I have several incarnations in common, and my granddaughter Angelia is literally the reincarnation of my cherished Grandma Ada. For my mother and me, on the other hand, this present life was more than enough time together, thank you, and my sister and I have had no previous acquaintance at all.

Some past-life relationships within a family can create positive, healthy, even tender present-tense dynamics. I have a client whose mother was her best friend in one previous life and her identical twin brother in another, and the bond between them to this day is nothing short of gorgeous. Another client was her own mother's mother in not one but two past lives. From the time this client was a small child, she's taken care of her chronically ill mother with extraordinary skill and compassion and not a hint of resentment, because, very accurately, it seems like the most natural thing in the world for her to do. Still another client has always idolized his father, and he wasn't particularly shocked when, during a regressive hypnosis session, we discovered that he and his father had served side by side in the Civil War and that his father had saved his life at Fort Sumter.

Other past-life connections within families can create grotesque situations. A case in point was a client named Danielle, who had an unspeakable childhood, sexually molested by her father from the age of five until he died when she was fifteen, while her mother blamed Danielle all her life for "letting it happen." Danielle, it turns out, was born in this life to a woman who despised her from a romantic rivalry in seventeenth-century France, and to a monstrous man who kidnapped her and sold her into slavery in the early 1830s.

So if we handpick every one of our family relationships, it's a breeze to understand why we choose the positive, nurturing ones. But why on earth would I choose an abusive, sociopathic mother, or would Danielle insist on such obscene and unforgivable parents? The answer to every question about the negative family members we've chosen is the same as the answer to all the other negativity we confront in this lifetime—we put it in our path to learn from it, overcome it, and let it help propel us toward our goals with even more strength and power. In my case, I can honestly say that my fierce commitment to be the finest, most protective mother I could possibly be was largely inspired by my childhood nightmare with the polar opposite of a fine, protective mother. As for Danielle, she has gone on to become one of the most tireless, passionate teachers and children's rights advocates I've ever met, hoping to save every defenseless child she can from the isolated hell she was subjected to.

Now, let's get something very, very straight: If you're an abusive parent, or if you're beyond the age of consent and are abusing, or allowing or deliberately ignoring the abuse of, a minor member of your family, there are a few things you can absolutely count on. One is that any success that minor child goes on to enjoy in life is in spite of you, not because of you, so don't even think about trying to pat yourself on the back or diminish the obscenity of what you're doing. Another is that, on the off chance you get through this life without severe consequences, you can read about the Dark Side in the "Guilt" chapter to find out what you have to look forward to when this life ends if you don't take *serious* steps to turn your behavior around. And still another is that if you wrote a chart that includes an impulse to mistreat members of your family, you wrote in that impulse so as to overcome it, not to indulge in it, no matter how much effort and help it takes to accomplish that.

"I'm Entitled to My Feelings"

I'm not telling you anything you don't know when I say that family relationships are about as complicated as any we'll ever face in our lives. Take it from me. In the chapter called "Discovering Life's Purpose" I discuss the option line we choose for each lifetime, which is the one area we need the most work on and find the hardest to get right no matter how hard we try. I chose "family" as my option line, and it shows. In fact, someday I'm sure I'll write at length about the timing of facing this particular chapter and how tempted I was to avoid it in this book. But no matter what your option line, families are an extraordinary phenomenon. Here are a group of people, all of whom handpicked each other before they arrived, some of whom have known each other time and time again, others of whom are complete strangers who may or may not ever feel a connection, all of whom know they're supposed to feel a connection because, after all, they're "blood," and all of whom chose each other for specific purposes without those purposes necessarily being compatible or obvious. If you look hard enough in any family, you'll find varying degrees of love, resentment, rivalry, respect, misunderstanding, courage, cowardice, tenderness, apathy, loyalty, betrayal, and both the best and worst treatment possible, every one of those ingredients magnified by sometimes voluntary and sometimes forced proximity. It's like everything we'll ever confront in society, all conveniently assembled in a group called "family," and there are no limits to what we can learn from them if we'll focus on exercising some of the same behavior with our families that we use with everyone else we meet along the way.

Families, for example, are the perfect place to examine that widely popular excuse for bad behavior, "I'm entitled to my feelings." We've always been incredibly interested in our own feelings, but somewhere along the line, especially during the "Me Decade" of the 1970s, we seem to have decided that our feelings are almost sacrosanct, earth-stoppingly important, worthy of our most intense scrutiny and our constant attention. We've been encouraged

to take pride in "being in touch with our feelings" to the point where we can't talk enough
about "our feelings," read enough about "our
feelings," write enough about "our feelings,"
and practically club people over the head
with "our feelings." Unfortunately, in all the
obsessing about "our feelings," someone
forgot to mention that *not all of our feelings
are appropriate, and not all of our feelings
have any business being acted on.* And that
fact is most often overlooked within families,
where proximity and familiarity create the
false impression that we can behave any way
we damn well please and let "our feelings"
dictate our treatment of each other.

It's a rare day in my office when I don't
meet a client who's clinging to the two defi-
ant claims "I'm entitled to my feelings" and
"I can't help it," and almost without exception they have no idea how much damage
they're doing to their family and, ultimately,
to themselves. Daren was a perfect example.
Married, three children, affluent, a valued
software developer in Silicon Valley. He
thought he wanted to discuss his deceased
father's missing will. I could see immediately
he had a more pressing problem, and I asked
if he was aware that his wife was seriously

considering taking their children and leaving him, not for another man but for a peaceful, emotionally stable life away from Daren's rude, short-tempered, often insulting moodiness. He couldn't have been more shocked. Sure, after a long, hard, stressful day at work, he might snap at his children when they got on his nerves, and, okay, he occasionally called his wife an "idiot" or an "airhead" when she screwed up around the house. But it was "normal." It was "his house," after all, and he "had a right" to blow off steam from so much career stress when he got home. Besides, he "couldn't help it." I asked him if he ever snapped when his boss got on his nerves. No. I asked him if he ever called his boss an idiot or an airhead when he screwed up. Of course not. And since it was his job that was creating most of his stress, did he ever blow off steam at the office? Don't be silly. "So if you're able to control your frustration until you get home, that means you *can* help it, right?" I asked him. He was silent, so I went on. "And if it's 'your right' to blow off steam because of all this job stress, why not exercise that right at work, where the problem is?" He allowed a half-laugh and answered, "Because nobody at work is obligated to put up with it."

In other words, in Daren's mind, and in most people's minds, our family *is* obligated to put up with it, to tolerate treatment we would never subject our boss, coworkers, friends, or even casual acquaintances to. Also, in Daren's and most other people's minds, the likely consequence of being rude, snappish, and temperamental at work is getting fired. But since our family can't get rid of us nearly that easily, all too often our behavior toward and around them doesn't seem worth checking.

Daren liked the majority of his coworkers. There were a few he thoroughly disliked. But even they received better treatment, more courtesy, and more patient consideration than his family, whom he loved and who loved him. And I don't need to be psychic to know how many of us are guilty of that same thing, saving our best efforts for the rest of the world and using our families as a dumping ground for all our moodiness and frustration. No wonder that tired adjective *dysfunctional* is so overused as a description for families that we've all started rolling our eyes every time we hear it. We're so busy flexing our entitled-to-our-feelings muscles and "not helping it" because we think our families are obligated to put up with it that our families end up trying to live with the worst, not the best, of who we are.

Again, there's not a single member of our family we didn't handpick to be related to, just as there's not a single member of our family who didn't handpick us. And we all handpicked each other for a reason, for some lesson that will be to our ultimate benefit if we'll pay attention and start with the assumption that everyone we're related to has a value specific to our goals for this lifetime. For that fact alone, every member of our family deserves the basic respect due anyone who's serving some purpose for us. Don't get me wrong, I'm not saying that we're obligated to like each and every one of our relatives. In fact, considering the variety of charts, past-life histories, lack of past-life histories, and priorities this time around that join together under the "family" heading, it's against the odds that we *will* all like each other. I'm not saying we're obligated to agree with each other on every issue, every choice, and every lifestyle because we're related. I'm not even saying we should let the word *family* hold us hostage to the point where we're required to accept the unacceptable and forgive the unforgivable. But I am saying that when it comes to just plain old basic manners, civility, and politeness, it's time we got back to *starting* with these people we chose to be related to, instead of expecting them to be satisfied with nothing but the loose change left over from the patient courtesy we've spent on everyone else.

For many of you, this will be the hardest exercise in this whole book, but I hope you'll give it a try, if only as an experiment to discover how much easier or how much more difficult it is than you would have expected. *I want you to choose one day a week, by mutual agreement, in which everyone in your family goes out of their way to be courteous and thoughtful toward each other. I'm not talking about undergoing major personality changes, I'm just talking about basics like saying "please," "thank you," and "you're welcome"; declaring name-calling, insults, arguments, and yelling off limits; paying a compliment; arriving home on time; asking "how are you?" and actually listening to the answer; looking for some small way to be helpful; calling a relative who's lonely or having problems just to ask if they're okay—*

again, just common, decent behavior, and frankly, I don't even care if you mean it, just go through the motions if that's the best you can do. If anyone doesn't care to participate, that's fine. Part of the challenge of this exercise is not to let someone else's bad behavior compromise the good behavior you've committed to for the day. For every infraction—every raised voice, every careless remark, every breach of politeness—the perpetrator has to deposit a quarter in a designated jar, with the eventual proceeds to be spent on something that will benefit the family, to be decided by a majority vote. One day a week for six months, and I guarantee the majority of you will be more than a little surprised at what a challenge it is and what a difference it can make.

And isn't one day a week of behaving decently toward your own family worth the effort, when in the end, you and the progress of the chart you wrote will reap the vast majority of the benefits?

A Few Words about Family Betrayal

I wish I didn't know a thing about betrayal within a family, and I wish it weren't a subject that comes up at least ten times a week during readings. If you've ever been on the receiving end of betrayal by a family member, you know that it cuts especially deep and that the repercussions can cause years' worth of pain and division among relatives whose loyalty and sense of fairness are put to tests they neither asked for nor deserved. And typically, the family bond that the betrayer was so willing to abuse for their own purpose is the same thing they'll try to use as leverage to demand understanding and forgiveness.

A client named Sarah illustrated that point beautifully. Her cousin Annie, whose car was about to be repossessed, borrowed $4,500 to satisfy the car loan, prevailing on Sarah's notorious devotion to their family in general when she asked for the money. Annie then made no effort whatsoever to repay the loan and complained to anyone in the family who would listen about Sarah's "harassment" in trying to recoup the money she was owed. Finally, after two years, when Annie hadn't repaid a single dime, Sarah took her to small claims court and won a judgment for the $4,500 she was entitled to, whereupon Annie began dividing the family into enemy camps, bringing up at every gathering what a disloyal lowlife Sarah was "to drag her own cousin into court over a measly $4,500." The fact that it was Sarah, not Annie, who was the real victim in this situation was largely lost in the translation, and for $4,500 a widespread family feud had been raging for almost a decade.

Sound familiar? I'd be very surprised if it doesn't. Based on my own experience and the experiences of thousands of clients over my forty-nine years of readings, family members taking outrageous advantage of each other and then expecting special dispensation for being "family" is horribly common. From unpaid loans to cheating with relatives' lovers or spouses to stealing to lying to dishonest greediness over estates and inheritances, it sadly seems that it's a very rare family in which someone hasn't crossed that boundary into outright betrayal, and the fact that it *is* family makes it even more excruciating to deal with than betrayal usually is.

If you're on the receiving end of a family betrayal, I hope you'll turn to the "Forgiveness" chapter and take it to heart, including the fact that some acts really are unforgivable and have to be given to God to handle, *even when the betrayer is a family member.* Writing betrayal into our chart means that our intention was to learn from it and ultimately profit from it, so the more we focus on that as our goal, our responsibility, and our eventual reward, and refuse to be held hostage by bloodlines, the less tempted we'll be to instigate family drama.

If you're the betrayer, on the other hand, sorry, but you can't point to your chart and say, "See? I couldn't help it, it was written into my chart before I even came here." Like everything else in your chart, all you wrote in was the situation, the opportunity to betray someone, for you to be either weak enough to stoop to or strong enough to pass up. If you choose to betray a family member, you fail a test you mapped out for yourself, and you've set yourself up for a lot of hard, guaranteed consequences ahead. And there's one consequence in particular that you'll learn sooner or later, no matter how much you might feel at the moment you got away with something: *There is no such thing as lasting happiness that has its roots in betrayal.*

Because a family member I love very much needs a special reminder of that fact right now about a betrayer, and frankly so do I, I hope you'll forgive my indulgence in repeating it for our benefit:

There is no such thing as lasting happiness that has its roots in betrayal.

Friends

Our yearning for friends—*real* friends, honest, loyal, and loving—is something we arrive with, from our rich and gorgeous lives full of friends at Home. On The Other Side, where the earthly version of the traditional family doesn't exist, our friends are our family, our companions, our confidants, our pleasure. They're the kindred souls with whom we share the joy of paradise and, very often, the rigors of earth as well, since some of us invariably decide to incarnate together, if only to remind each other of Home when we run into each other here in boot camp and then share a good laugh about it when we're back on The Other Side again.

The tricky thing is, we're very spoiled on The Other Side by the simple fact that it's impossible to make wrong choices when it comes to friendships. Where there are no dark entities, no egos, no ulterior motives, no jealousies, no urges to compete or use or take advantage or manipulate, there is no risk of choosing our friends badly. We're naturally drawn to entities with whom we share common interests, senses of humor, and goals, but when it comes to picking loving friends who live with honor and integrity, everyone we can close our eyes and point to at Home will have those qualities.

Needless to say, if you'll forgive the understatement, we don't exactly have that luxury here. It just takes us a while to figure that out—sometimes, come to think of it, about fifty or sixty years—and to realize that true friends on earth are rare, that the quality of our friends is much more important than the quantity, and that those few real friends we'll find during our lifetime are worth the sometimes painful search, and even worth the mistakes we'll inevitably make along the way.

Just as we handpick our family members when we compose our chart, we also handpick our friends, both the genuine ones and, let's face it, the losers. We write them in for the same reasons we write in everything else, good and bad, joy and sorrow, success and failure: to learn, to grow, and to make progress along the eternal path of our spirit. And one of the Catch-22's of discerning between the friends we're meant to embrace on earth and those we're meant to walk away from is that, because we forecast them all in our chart, we can experience the same immediate recognition, the same familiarity, the same "There you are!" for both kinds, without knowing at first which is which. Learning to tell them apart is a lesson we often have to learn the hard way, like most lessons of lasting value.

Logically, it should be easy for us to spot a poor choice of friends, because friendships typically don't go through that same best-behavior stage that almost always characterize potential romantic relationships. In fact, one of the definitions of a friend is someone with whom we can completely relax and be ourselves, warts and all. So it's not as if we're not given all the hints we need and more about the character of a person we're befriending. It's just that, unless we're really paying attention, we're likely to pay more attention to the there-you-are! phenomenon than we are to the signals telling us whether to pursue the friendship or run screaming.

"You should meet my friend Joe," we might say, chuckling. "What a character. He can scam anything he wants out of anyone." Or "My friend Mary's a lot of fun, but she can't seem to keep her hands off of other people's husbands." Or "I love my friend Denise, she knows all the best gossip on all our other friends." Or "My buddy Nick couldn't tell the truth if his life depended on it." Or "Good old Billy, he has a perfectly good job, but he's declared bankruptcy twice." And then Joe scams *us,* or Mary makes a pass at *our* husband, or Denise talks about us behind *our* back, or Nick lies to *us,* or we loan Billy money and he never pays *us* back, and we couldn't be more shocked and hurt.

Here are a couple of tips that could help you speed your chart back on track again when you find yourself struggling with a friendship dilemma. First, and always, *be discerning ahead of time, not after the fact.* Remember, no matter what our specific goals are for this lifetime, our greatest general challenge is to overcome the negativity we came here to confront, so honoring it with our time and the cherished label of "friend" is guaranteed to throw us off track.

Second, imagine the boost to our chart, and maybe even the chart of a friend whose questionable values are coming between us, if we were to declare and enforce "house rules" with that friend—essentially, tell them that what they do around other people is their business, but if our friendship is going to survive, the scams/betrayal/gossip/lies/unpaid loans have to be off limits between us. By setting up house rules, we make it clear how important our values are to us, and it becomes their choice whether they want to comply with our house rules or move on. Either way, with them or without them, we're making an important statement to our sacred, cherished God-center: We can't be a friend or earn a friend by demanding anything less than our finest from ourselves and from each other.

The Exercise

I want you to feel yourself walking in a field bright with flowers. A soft wind blows, carrying with it the joyful sound of distant birds and the sweet, delicate smell of lilac. The sun is high and warm on your face, and it exhilarates you. Your pace quickens with the rare pleasure of how alive, how peaceful, and how safe you feel with each new sure step on the soft grass. There's no one around, and you cherish the freedom of your solitude.

You stop to rest in an arbor of jasmine, its graceful arms wrapping gently around you to welcome you to its comforting bed of green and white. Your mind and body release their tightness, their stress, their worries, their pain. Your breathing slows and deepens. Utterly content, briefly noticing that the sun is lower in the sky and coloring its azure blue with faint tendrils of pink, you let your eyes close, and you fall into a restful sleep.

You open your eyes again, startled awake by a sudden unpleasant awareness that the warm breeze has turned to a cold and ominous wind, warning of a gathering storm. You stand, shivering, and look around, no longer comforted by your solitude but feeling alone and afraid and so small in this endless expanse of darkness. Your logical mind assures you that God is with you, and your Spirit Guide and Angels are with you, but you yearn for the firm touch of a human hand to take yours and lead you toward some distant safety. Frightened, you take a few uncertain steps on the cold, wet grass, and it occurs to you that, at least for the moment in this black night, you've lost your way. You release a cry for help, but your voice is drowned by a mean rumble of thunder.

You're looking around with growing panic when suddenly, for an instant, a white half-moon appears through a break in the clouds, and in its brief light you see a small group of people assembling around you, shadows at first, but their faces, their eyes, are illuminated just enough for you to recognize that familiar help has come. Not everyone you might have hoped for. Not everyone you might have expected. But in the warmth as they encircle you and shield you from the wind you hear their silent reassurance. "I am your sister. I am your grandfather. I am your friend, your mother, your brother. I know you, without words or judgments, and as we have done for thousands of years, or as we'll do for the first time now, we will keep each other safe and find our way home together."

A strong hand takes yours. A comforting arm envelops your shoulders. This small, cherished, familiar circle closes around you as the clouds seem to melt away, leaving the brilliant moon and a blanket of stars behind to shine on a wide, clear path away from danger, away from your desolate solitude, away from the fear that gripped you when you thought you had to bear it all alone. Together you start down the path, protected, protecting in return, in no hurry anymore as you realize that in the security of this help that knew to come and share the darkness, you've already found your way home.

THE AFFIRMATION

"Throughout this day, may I remember that the light of my spirit shines at its strongest when I use it to brighten the path of the family and friends I chose to share this brief part of my eternal journey."

The Holidays

Or, as many people prefer to call them, "the hell-idays" . . .

I've often said, if being alone on major holidays depresses you, come spend the holidays at my house and listen to my family fight. Trust me, you'll leave *yearning* to be alone. That's not to say there's anything uniquely dysfunctional (I'm so tired of that word) about my family. Some of us are crazy about each other. Some of us are just crazy. Some of us shouldn't be in the same room, let alone in the same family, with each other. But every year, on prescribed occasions, as if we're hostages to the calendar, we dutifully assemble, exchange gifts nobody needs, drink eggnog nobody likes, and try to pretend that we're all problem free and that we're not all stressed out, traveled out, shopped out, spent out, caroled out, malled out, gift-wrapped out, decorated out, cooked out, and secretly wishing for privacy, a nice hot bath, and about five days' sleep.

You don't need me to tell you that the holidays—any holidays—can be difficult. You're already well aware that they're overly commercialized, and that we're having Christmas in particular shoved in our faces earlier every year, to the point where I won't be surprised if children start to believe "Silent Night" and "Deck the Halls" are traditional Halloween shopping songs. You know that the suicide rate jumps around the holidays, and it probably won't surprise you that urgent calls to my office for help and reassurance quadruple between Thanksgiving and January 1. There are increases in crime, traffic accidents, and drunk-driving arrests, as well as in incidents of domestic violence and assaults. Not exactly what anyone had in mind, I'm sure, as the ideal way to wish Jesus a happy birthday or welcome in a new year or honor our war veterans.

I certainly don't mean to ignore those of you out there who love the holidays, and I want you to know that the rest of us applaud you and hate you. (I'm kidding. Kind of.) And I'm convinced that happy holidays and miserable ones occur for the very same reason: Holidays have a way of shining a spotlight on our lives, good and bad, past and present, in a glare of added intensity, with the help of a barrage of unavoidable reminders of what day it is and a subtle message from the world around us that somehow, on these arbitrary occasions, we're obliged to be in a great mood or be judged completely inappropriately. If life is going well and our memories of any given holiday are primarily fond ones, chances are we'll be ready and eager to celebrate. But if times are tough, or our memories make us want to hide under the bed and not come out until the celebrating is over with, the festivities going on around us feel mocking and hollow.

Again, depending on the circumstances, any holiday can trigger sadness, no matter how hard we try to grin and bear our way through it. My cowriter, Lindsay, has suffered the death of three important loved ones at Christmastime and would like nothing more than to find a way to fast-forward from about mid-November until the first week of January. I lost my daddy at Easter, and just the innocuous sight of colored eggs and chocolate bunnies makes my heart ache, not to mention the emptiness that still invariably hits every Father's Day. I have a client for whom every Mother's Day marks the anniversary of her mother's vengeful suicide. Another client lost his fiancée to an accidental drowning one Thanksgiving day and his best friend to AIDS exactly a year later. Examples of holiday-related tragedies among my family, friends, and clients go on and on and on.

And then there are those for whom holidays are simply reminders that times are tough and there's not much to celebrate no matter what the calendar says. Financial problems, illness, homelessness, being separated from family and friends, any sense of loss or disruption, can cause as much of a sense of dread around the holidays as the death of someone we love. In fact, to be perfectly honest, thanks to the horrendous ordeal my family and I have been through this year, I announced months ago that while I'll go to any lengths to make things as fun and normal for my grandchildren as possible, I'm boycotting Christmas until further notice. No gifts, to or from anyone over the age of twelve. No decorating. No getting up before dawn to get the turkey in the oven in time to eat it the same day I started it. As few carols as humanly possible. Come to think of it, I may just herd the whole group of us off to some quiet foreign resort where it won't be as painfully apparent that things at home are not the same anymore.

Will I feel guilty or disrespectful not celebrating the birth of Christ? Not a chance. I do that 365 days a year, as best I can, in the way I live. Which I really believe, given a choice between that and running ourselves ragged burying ourselves under a mountain of credit card bills, He'd prefer from all of us anyway.

I'll also continue to follow the advice I always give to my clients about getting through this time of year with as much grace and as little anxiety as possible. Whether holidays fill you with dread or with joy and excitement, I hope you'll find something in the next pages that will be comforting, useful, and maybe even worth adding to your own annual traditions.

Survival Tips for the Holidays

- I would love for you to do this every morning of your life and every night before you sleep, but I want you to make a special point of it before, during, and after every holiday: Give yourself added spiritual protection from the heightened negativity that's inevitable at times of heightened emotions. Surround yourself and your loved ones with the white light of the Holy Spirit. Then, in your mind, build a perfect circle of mirrors around yourself, all facing outward, that will move with you wherever you go. As long as you're inside that circle of mirrors, any negativity that approaches, instead of having access to you, will be reflected back into itself and, repelled by its own ugliness, shrink away in defeat, leaving you unharmed.
- Years ago I made a pact with my close friends and adult family members that has been a big relief to all of us, financially and emotionally, and I can't recommend it strongly enough. Very

simply, we agreed not to exchange holiday gifts. Period. We focus that money and energy instead on trying to make the holidays as magical for the children as we can, in an effort to give them memories to cherish that will last far longer than any gift we could possibly buy. And then, during the year, when the pressure is off and we're motivated by love rather than obligation, we adults give each other gifts either on our birthdays or for no occasion at all.

- There's a gorgeous tradition that will make you feel better than you can imagine and teach your children a lovely lesson they can use throughout their lives. Pick an evening two or three weeks before the holidays and gather your family around a supply of wrapping paper, boxes, and ribbon. Then each of you choose one item you've enjoyed from among your own belongings, gift wrap it, and anonymously deliver them all to a nearby homeless shelter, rescue mission, hospice, needy family, or local school or hospital for them to give at their discretion where they'll be most appreciated.

- If there are no children around you, include a toy in your holiday shopping anyway, and take it to a children's home or pediatric ward at the nearest hospital, where I promise you there's a child for whom the simplest gesture on your part can make all the difference in the world. And if, like all of us from time to time, you have no extra money to spend, give your time and your heart instead. Those same children would love for you to read to them, or play games with them, or just talk with and listen to them, as a reminder to them and to us that children—all children— are the most divine human beings on earth and deserve to be actively cherished and honored by every one of us.
- Speaking of earth's divine citizens, don't ever forget the animals, especially around the holidays. If you're not blessed enough to be able to adopt a pet of your own, *please* deliver or arrange to have delivered a supply of however much food you can afford to an animal shelter, humane society, or rescue organization.
- Remember, you don't ever have to be

alone for the holidays if you don't want to be. There are shelters, missions, and charities all around you who need volunteers every day of the year and especially on those days when many people are too busy traveling and celebrating to find an extra moment for anyone but themselves.

- If someone you know is going to be alone for the holidays, include them in your plans and assure them how welcome they'll be, but remember to let it be their choice, without pressure, whether to join you or not. I've had the experience, and I'm sure you have, too, of feeling more alone in a roomful of acquaintances than I would have if I'd stayed home by myself, and that feeling can become even more intense at times when we're told we're supposed to be surrounded by family and friends.

- The holidays are *not* a time to be shy about asking for help. There's no shame in being depressed, or anxious, or lonely, or financially strapped, and I promise you, if any or all of those things are true, you have a lot more company around you than you might have been led to believe. Please run, don't walk, to a doctor, therapist, support group, free clinic, pastor, rabbi, counselor, or my own amazing staff of ministers, all of whom have been trained not just to see you through these challenging days but that you actually emerge from them stronger, healthier, more vital, and feeling more blessed than you've ever felt before. Again, you can reach my ministers twenty-four hours a day through my office at (408) 379-7070 or through the Internet at my Web site, www.sylvia.org. They'll never solicit you for membership or for a single dime, they'll just deeply care and be there for you whenever you need them.

- With all due respect to mail-order companies who sell fruitcake, cheese baskets, fruit-of-the-month, giant bars of chocolate, decorative tins of popcorn, and a year's supply of floral arrangements, wouldn't it be great to see, if only for one holiday season, the same money spent on that usually mindless list of catalog orders donated instead to the intended recipients' favorite charities?

- And last but not least, if the holidays are a time of special joy and prosperity for you, let them also be a time when you challenge your spirit to its greatest heights of humility, gratitude, and generosity, so that not a day of celebration passes without your thanking God for your many blessings by extending your hand and heart to the smallest, the neediest, and the most helpless of His children. His thanks to you in return will only multiply your joy and prosperity, giving you even more to share day after day, year after year, through the rest of the eternity He's promised us all.

THE AFFIRMATION

"Dearest Lord,

"Again another Christmastime—a celebration of God's love that came into life. Rather than congratulations on Your birthday, or promises that we make above what we can fulfill—we ask that out of all the tinsel and commercialism, we can emulate your life all year long.

"That the gift that we give You is to find our own God-center and live a life of example that You conveyed to us so simplistically over two thousand years ago.

"That we evolve toward our own perfection and not allow ourselves to complicate our lives with guilts and regrets.

"That as You taught, we find our temple of the Holy Spirit within ourselves.

"Your gift to us was to love ourselves, and like any gift, we should show our appreciation by wearing our souls proudly, so that when we stand before You, we can be proud of the gift of ourselves—we can give back to you clean hearts, spiritually strong and filled with love.

"Your present to us was not only Your birth, but Your life. How ungrateful if we did not try it on, fit it to us, and wear it with pride until we can all meet and be united in God's love. Amen."

In Closing

May your life be enriched every minute of every day by blessings not only from The Other Side but also from the bottom of my grateful heart. I wish you joy. I wish you peace. I wish you warmth from the flame of the God-center that burns eternally in your spirit, and light from that flame for all to see. Until we meet again, here on earth or in the divine paradise of Home—

God loves you. I do.

SYLVIA C. BROWNE

About the Author

Sylvia Browne is the best-selling author of *Life on The Other Side, The Other Side and Back,* and *Adventures of a Psychic.* A working psychic for almost fifty years, Ms. Browne regularly appears on *The Montel Williams Show.*

You can find out more about Sylvia Browne through her Web site:

www.sylvia.org